Instant Messaging Reference

## Chandos
### Information Professional Series

Series Editor: Ruth Rikowski
(e-mail: Rikowskigr@aol.com)

Chandos' new series of books are aimed at the busy information professional. They have been specially commissioned to provide the reader with an authoritative view of current thinking. They are designed to provide easy-to-read and (most importantly) practical coverage of topics that are of interest to librarians and other information professionals. If you would like a full listing of current and forthcoming titles, please visit our website **www.chandospublishing.com** or contact Hannah Grace-Williams on e-mail info@chandospublishing.com or telephone number +44 (0) 1993 848726.

**New authors:** we are always pleased to receive ideas for new titles; if you would like to write a book for Chandos, please contact Dr Glyn Jones on e-mail gjones@chandospublishing.com or telephone number +44 (0) 1993 848726.

**Bulk orders:** some organisations buy a number of copies of our books. If you are interested in doing this, we would be pleased to discuss a discount. Please contact Hannah Grace-Williams on e-mail info@chandospublishing.com or telephone number +44 (0) 1993 848726.

# Instant Messaging Reference: A practical guide

RACHEL BRIDGEWATER
AND
MERYL B. COLE

Chandos Publishing
*Oxford · England*

Chandos Publishing (Oxford) Limited
TBAC Business Centre
Avenue 4
Station Lane
Witney
Oxford OX28 4BN
UK
Tel: +44 (0) 1993 848726 Fax: +44 (0) 1865 884448
E-mail: info@chandospublishing.com
**www.chandospublishing.com**

---

First published in Great Britain in 2009

ISBN:
978 1 84334 357 8 (paperback)
978 1 84334 358 5 (hardback)
1 84334 357 6 (paperback)
1 84334 358 4 (hardback)



British Library Cataloguing-in-Publication Data.
A catalogue record for this book is available from the British Library.



Typeset by Domex e-Data Pvt. Ltd.
Printed in the UK and USA.

# Contents

# List of figures and tables

## Figures

## Tables

# About the authors

**Rachel Bridgewater** is an academic librarian living in Portland, Oregon. She is currently the electronic resources librarian at Reed College. Prior to joining the staff at Reed in 2008, Rachel was the reference coordinator at Washington State University Vancouver library. In both libraries she initiated and coordinated instant messaging reference service as a way of extending reference service beyond the desk.

A frequent speaker at library conferences, Rachel strives to help library audiences understand how social software and media are changing the information landscape in which they operate. She also speaks, writes and teaches about copyright policy.

Rachel writes about library and information policy issues at http://command-f.info. In her spare time, Rachel runs around Portland.

**Meryl B. Cole** came to librarianship from a wide-ranging background in teaching and corporate communications. Her work in distinct and diverse communities – university, community college, corporate America and international school – shapes her thought process and encourages her to think broadly. After becoming a librarian in 2005, Meryl worked as a reference librarian at Washington State University in Vancouver.

Throughout her career Meryl's focus has been singular: impart and share information in a variety of ways and experiment with a variety of methods. The appeal of IM reference for Meryl is that it is both an alternative and an additional method, not replacing but augmenting traditional approaches to reference.

Meryl believes in the vitality of librarianship in today's increasingly wired world. The strength of the profession lies in librarians' resilience and resourcefulness.

# Acknowledgements

Our heartfelt thanks go to all of the talented librarians who contributed their first-person experiences using IM. These narratives enrich the book tremendously.

- Josh Boyer, North Carolina State University, Pam Sessoms, University of North Carolina at Chapel Hill and Amy VanScoy, North Carolina State University.
- Karen Diller, currently assistant vice chancellor of academic affairs at Washington State University Vancouver.
- Jason Eiseman, librarian at the law firm of Schwabe, Williamson & Wyatt.
- Kate Gronemyer, reference and instructional librarian at Oregon State University Cascades Library.
- Erica Carlson Nicol, electronic resources librarian at the Holland and Terrell Libraries of Washington State University Pullman.
- Jenna Ryan, science reference librarian at the Middleton Library at Louisiana State University.
- Caleb Tucker-Raymond, project coordinator for the Oregon Statewide Reference program, L-Net.

*Rachel.* I am grateful to all my mentors, who have encouraged me to try new things, think new thoughts and experiment with new approaches to service. With thanks especially to Karen Diller, Dena Hutto, Perri Parise, Carrie Russell and Anne-Marie Deitering. Thanks, as always, to Jason.

*Meryl.* Much love and many thanks to my family and friends for it all. For Roger, my champion, and Violet and Birch, my superstars, dino-sized smoochie-bodoochies forever.

# List of acronyms

| | |
|---|---|
| AIM | AOL Instant Messenger |
| ALA | American Library Association |
| AOL | America Online |
| ARL | Association of Research Libraries |
| EIM | enterprise instant messaging |
| FAQ | frequently asked question |
| FSU | Florida State University |
| HIPAA | Health Insurance Portability and Accounting Act (USA) |
| IM | instant messaging |
| IPL | Internet Public Library |
| IRC | Internet Relay Chat |
| IT | information technology |
| LSU | Louisiana State University |
| NCSU | North Carolina State University |
| OCLC | Online Computer Library Center |
| OTR | Off-the-Record |
| PGP | Pretty Good Privacy |
| RUSA | ALA Reference and User Services Association |
| SMS | short message service |
| SMTP | Simple Messaging and Transfer Protocol |
| SSL | Secure Socket Layer |
| SSN | social security number |
| ULC | Urban Libraries Council |
| UNC | University of North Carolina at Chapel Hill |

| | |
|---|---|
| VR | virtual reference |
| WSU | Washington State University |
| XML | eXtensible Markup Language |
| XMPP | Extensible Messaging and Presence Protocol |

1

# Introduction

Over the course of the last five years or so, more and more libraries have been discovering instant messaging (IM) as an easy, effective, low- or no-cost way of providing virtual reference services. This book is intended to help librarians, especially those with little or no personal experience with IM, get answers to their questions about IM in general and IM reference in particular. Though the software is easy to use and the barriers to entry are low, librarians like to approach new services carefully and thoughtfully, armed with the answers and solutions to all potential questions and problems. We hope this book will give you the background you need to introduce IM reference services confidently in your library.

We begin the book with an overview of virtual reference. It is important to place IM reference in this broader context at the outset. Many of us have experience of using a variety of web-based chat products for virtual reference or have read about the strengths and weaknesses of such systems over the years. IM shares some qualities in common with such services but is substantially different. When presenting at conferences about IM reference or talking to colleagues informally, one question that seems to come up time and time again is 'Which is better – "traditional" virtual reference (web-based chat products like QuestionPoint) or IM?' We hope to demonstrate at the outset that this question misses the point. IM and web-based chat tools fill different needs. Both have strengths and weaknesses, and there are cases where you might choose to use both! It is a bit like asking 'Which is better – telephone reference or e-mail reference?' Neither is inherently preferable, they're just different.

Many fine books and articles have been written about virtual reference over the years, and we don't hope to replicate that work here. So Chapter 2 seeks only to bring all readers up to speed with the basics of virtual reference. We provide some basic history, a short justification for the use of virtual reference and a brief comparison of the basic options for providing virtual reference.

Chapter 3 delves into the basics of IM. Though IM is ridiculously easy to use, it is actually quite helpful to understand a bit of what is happening behind the scenes when you chat via IM. This chapter explains both 'what' and 'why' of IM – providing a short history of IM and demonstrating its popularity, especially among younger users. We also explain the 'how' of IM. How does it work? How is it like or unlike e-mail? How does the technology behind IM introduce complexity into an IM reference service? What is the relationship between the software you use for IM and the account/network you use to access the service? It is our hope that, after reading Chapter 3, you will have a firm understanding of IM protocols and clients that will serve you well as you make decisions about your IM reference service.

Once you get the basics under your belt, you'll be ready to get started. Chapter 4 provides nuts-and-bolts information about establishing user names on the various IM networks, choosing and setting up an IM client, staffing your service, providing training for your colleagues and establishing the necessary policy framework to support the service.

Is providing a reference interview over IM different to conducting one in person? Yes and no. Many librarians who have never used IM or never provided virtual reference services worry that IM reference interactions will be impersonal, difficult, awkward or otherwise unpleasant. In our experience, IM interactions can be very much like face-to-face interactions – which is no guarantee that they will all be pleasant, of course! In Chapter 5 we outline the basic steps involved with negotiating a reference question in IM. Armed with a little bit of background, a little bit of experience and a positive attitude, IM reference can be fun and, more importantly, highly effective.

The success of your IM reference service will be determined to some degree by your ability to meet and manage the expectations of your patrons and staff. Both patrons and staff will come to your service with their unique experiences, attitudes and expectations. While you can't please everyone all the time, putting some thought into managing expectations can improve your chances of success. We also provide, in Chapter 6, a comprehensive look at the literature regarding staff attitudes towards IM and virtual reference. Understanding possible staff reactions can help you address these issues head on.

As time goes on, you'll want to evaluate and update your IM service. Chapter 7 provides some basic guidelines for service evaluation. Again, countless works have been written about the evaluation of services – examining surveys, focus groups and other evaluation tools in depth. We don't hope to replicate those works here, just to provide some general guidelines and ideas.

In Chapter 8 we take on advanced topics in IM reference. If you're interested in using website widgets to embed IM in your site, this is the chapter that will explain the ins and outs of widgets. We also look at enterprise IM and the promising emerging world of collaborative IM reference.

IM is not without its issues and problems. Librarians proposing to introduce IM reference services in their organizations should be prepared to face questions about security, privacy, harassment and scalability, among others. Most of the issues presented by IM can be easily solved with some combination of common sense, policy and technology. In Chapter 9 we detail the possible issues and problems surrounding IM, and propose solutions to those problems where possible.

Finally, we close the book with some thoughts about promoting and marketing your IM reference service. After all, your service won't be used if your patrons aren't aware that it exists!

Throughout this book you'll find insightful, first-person narratives from librarians detailing their experiences with IM. Erica Carlson Nicol, electronic resources librarian at the Holland and Terrell Libraries of Washington State University Pullman, provides a detailed narrative of their implementation of IM reference. Erica explains how they decided to start the service, the steps they took to get it going and how they publicized the service. Erica gives excellent insight into the process that a large academic library undertakes when it decides to launch IM. To provide a view of the steps a small library takes when setting up an IM service, we asked Kate Gronemyer, reference and instructional librarian at Oregon State University Cascades Library, to describe her experiences. Jenna Ryan, science reference librarian at the Middleton Library at Louisiana State University, posted a richly detailed yet very understandable explanation of the LSU IM set-up to the DIG-REF list-serv and we knew we had to have it in this book. Jenna graciously agreed to allow us to include it. Karen Diller, currently the assistant vice chancellor of academic affairs at Washington State University Vancouver, writes about how workplace communication changed at the WSU Vancouver library after some of the librarians started using IM for internal communications, highlighting just one of the cultural issues that can emerge with the introduction of IM into an organization. Workplace culture is only one of the issues you'll confront when you introduce IM: Jason Eiseman, librarian at the law firm of Schwabe, Williamson & Wyatt, describes the security and legal issues raised by IM. Finally, we were lucky enough to get contributions from leaders in the field for our chapter on advanced IM topics. Caleb Tucker-Raymond, project coordinator for the Oregon Statewide Reference program, L-Net, shares his expertise about enterprise IM and the XMPP protocol. For our feature about the LibraryH3lp collaborative IM project, we were fortunate to get a contribution from the developers of LibraryH3lp, Josh Boyer, North Carolina State University, Pam Sessoms, University of North Carolina at Chapel Hill, and Amy VanScoy, North Carolina State University. These first-person perspectives are included to enrich the work with the personal stories of librarians facing the same issues you will encounter as you seek to implement IM reference in your organization.

We hope this book will give you the information you need to start up a truly world-class IM reference service – one that meets the needs of your own unique community, that is embraced enthusiastically by your colleagues, that grows and changes based on effective evaluation, that confronts the problems inherent in IM head on and that you promote effectively and enthusiastically. Used effectively, IM will allow you to reach new patrons who have been underserved by traditional reference service and to reach existing patrons in new ways. The world of IM is changing all the time, but with a solid understanding of the basics and an appreciation of where IM fits in the overall set of services offered by your library, you'll be ready to face those changes!

2

# Virtual reference: an overview and brief history

> A learning society requires that we do more than develop the hardware, software, telecommunications networks, and other services and systems that supply and catalog content. It requires additional structure and context to enable learners around the globe to put knowledge to good use. And I think that virtual reference services are an important part of that process. (Martin, 2004: 225)

Though the subject of this book is specifically instant messaging reference, we feel it's important to spend some time at the beginning discussing 'virtual' reference in general. Looking at the evolution and development of virtual reference service since the 1990s will help place IM reference in context. Indeed, one of the first questions we're often asked about IM reference goes something like 'Which is better: IM reference or chat/virtual reference using virtual reference software?' The answer is, of course, neither is necessarily better – they serve useful purposes in many cases. It's important to remember that, as with so many things, it's not necessary to think of your IM reference service as an either/or. Just as we didn't give up phone reference when we started e-mail reference, starting IM reference doesn't mean you'll give up e-mail reference, for example. So, then, what do we mean when we talk about 'virtual reference'?

Virtual reference services, in the form of e-mail, appeared as far back as the early 1980s (Gross et al., 2001), but use really started expanding in the mid-1990s. It was around this time that we began thinking of virtual reference as 'person-to-person' reference via web forms, web-based chat and IM and 'user' reference via web tools provided on library websites (such as FAQs or internet resource gateways), not simply answering questions via e-mail.

An early player in the virtual reference world, the Internet Public Library (IPL) opened its doors in 1995. Started by the School of Information and Library Studies at the University of Michigan, the IPL is now hosted by Drexel University and is a consortium. The IPL is subject-directory based with an additional strong page of FAQs, also organized by subject. A forerunner in the virtual reference arena, the IPL is significant for its longevity (13 years old) and its reach – close to 1,000 library websites provide a link to the IPL (Crosby, 2007). The IPL also provides a web form for patrons to send in questions (Figure 2.1).

The IPL's form is a fine illustration of an online, asynchronous reference interview. Just as we do in an in-person reference interview, the IPL includes questions regarding the patron's planned use for the information and sources consulted. Recognizing the virtual nature of its service, the IPL asks where the patron lives so as to provide resources that best fit the information need. With its online subject directories and question form, the IPL was a pioneer and remains a productive presence in virtual reference.

## What is virtual reference?

To answer the question 'what is virtual reference?' it helps to start with a brief look at reference itself. According to the

**Figure 2.1** The Internet Public Library's web form

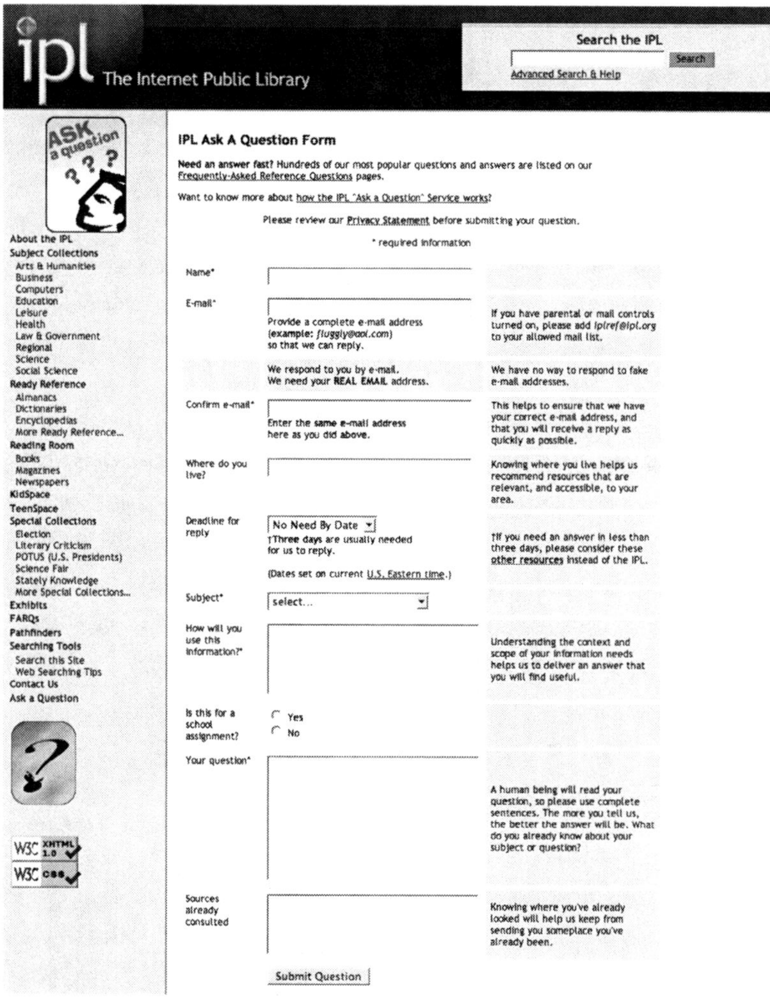


Association of Research Libraries (ARL), 'A reference transaction is an information contact that involves the knowledge, use, recommendations, interpretation, or instruction in the use of one or more information sources by a member of the library staff' (Kyrillidou and Young, 2006). Implicit in this definition is the face-to-face nature of traditional reference. This personal element of reference work has been part and parcel of reference. It defined reference – until recently. Technology has now driven a redefinition of reference, in the sense that face to face has now become person to person.

These new forms of person-to-person reference do not lend themselves to a standard definition, since the practice is still young and even the name is not set in stone. The variants – virtual, digital, e-, chat and live – all share the same general premise: electronic provision of reference service. For this book, we adopted the American Library Association (ALA) Reference and User Services Association's (RUSA) definition:

> 1.1 Virtual reference is reference service initiated electronically, often in real-time, where patrons employ computers or other Internet technology to communicate with reference staff, without being physically present. Communication channels used frequently in virtual reference include chat, videoconferencing, Voice over IP, co-browsing, e-mail, and instant messaging.
>
> 1.2 While online sources are often utilized in provision of virtual reference, use of electronic sources in seeking answers is not of itself virtual reference.
>
> 1.3 Virtual reference queries are sometimes followed-up with telephone, fax, in-person and regular mail interactions, even though these modes of communication are not considered virtual. (American Library Association, 2004)

We appreciate three elements of RUSA's definition. First, it is inclusive. Videoconferencing, voice over IP and co-browsing are included in addition to the main three modes of chat, e-mail and instant messaging. Second, although electronic sources may be provided by way of an answer, that alone is not enough to classify the interaction as virtual. And finally, RUSA's definition indicates that more traditional reference methods can be used in tandem with virtual reference services without nullifying the virtual classification.

Where RUSA's definition is straightforward and basic, others have a wider interpretation of activities that constitute virtual reference; these are worthy of consideration as we consider the future, keeping in mind how technology continues to change reference work. Lipow (2003: xix) summarizes the ideas of those who appreciate the role technology plays in reference's future and believe that virtual reference 'encompasses a broad range of electronic reference activities that include creating and managing digital reference resources (digitizing paper materials, producing original digital resources that have no paper counterpart, making available such electronic resources created elsewhere, constructing FAQ files, and such)'. This is both interesting and somewhat challenging, as it compels librarians to provide increasingly virtual overall services while still maintaining the face-to-face nature of reference work and providing quality service.

Boss (undated) echoes elements of Lipow's description: 'Virtual reference, also known as e-reference, is online reference service that assists patrons by placing answers to frequently asked questions (FAQs) on a library's Web site, mounting selected reference tools, providing an e-mail address or Web form for library patrons to ask reference questions, and/or providing real-time assistance using chat or instant messaging software.' Person-to-person reference service is only one facet of virtual reference, according to Boss. Librarians, virtual or not, have always worked to provide as many upfront resources as possible to empower patrons to locate credible information on their own. As Ferguson and Bunge (1997: 263) recognize: 'Reference service also places value on freedom of choice for the library's clients. Librarians help them realize their own goals, rather than forcing them to use information sources on the library's terms.'

Collaboration rounds out the definition of virtual reference. Just as many libraries belong to consortia and share lending, many libraries providing virtual reference belong to collaboratives and consortia, where libraries share provision of reference services.

## Why virtual reference?

Having briefly looked at definitions of reference and virtual reference, let's take a moment to explain why we think that virtual reference is a valuable addition to your reference services. Librarians provide reference, basically, to connect people with information – to bridge an information gap. There are various standard reference guides that provide thorough and theoretical explanations as to reference's purpose (Katz, 2002; Bopp and Smith, 2001). For our uses, Janes's (2004: 6–7) succinct explanation works:

> The preferred outcome is this: understand users and communities and their information needs, think hard and creatively about the nature of the information services that will help them to meet those needs, and then plan those services in such a way that they will succeed. The best reference services have always done precisely that.

It behoves us to plan services that match our communities' needs. Just as adding videotapes, audiobooks and DVDs to our collections recognized community needs, just as adding computers to our libraries recognized community needs, so too does implementing virtual reference services recognize community needs.

Why provide virtual reference services?

- Why not?
- Patrons of all ages are increasingly on the internet.
- To personalize the internet experience.
- To reach patrons who might not otherwise be reachable.
- To maintain a competitive edge in the information arena.
- To provide, and continue providing, quality service.

## *Why not?*

As you will see in the coming chapters, virtual reference can be a very easy, extremely low-cost way to extend services to previously unserved or underserved patrons and enhance services to patrons you are already serving well. Given this, we might rather ask: 'Why not provide some form of virtual reference service?' We can liken our virtual reference offerings to a retailer choosing to sell its wares online. When businesses launched websites to sell their products, they did not opt to close their physical locations. Rather, the online stores are viewed as just another avenue of service; just another option for their customers. Virtual reference service is simply that – another avenue of service.

## *Patrons of all ages are increasingly on the internet*

Reference transaction statistics, technology use and demographics all point to an audience for reference that is increasingly online. Traditional (non-virtual) reference statistics are down; according to the ARL, as of 2005 they were down nearly 50 per cent since 1991 (Kryillidou and

Young, 2006: 8). Clearly, reference librarians are no longer reaching their audience as they once did.

Lipow (2002, 2003: 8) strongly advocates a more proactive approach for reference librarians, eschewing the reference desk as a 'just in case' method of providing reference. The internet is where, she believes, reference librarians should be: 'Moving the reference desk out to the internet places the librarian where the clients are: amid the chaotic information landscape, a far better place to be as a bridge to quality information.' While there are those who would debate whether the internet is 'a better place to be', much of the evidence indicates that it is certainly one of the places librarians must be.

Studies from the Pew Internet & American Life Project and the Urban Libraries Council bear out Lipow's belief. According to Pew (2008), while the definition of who uses the internet has changed slightly over the years – from accessing computer bulletin boards in 1995 to occasional use of the internet in 2005 – the percentage of adults (over 18 as defined by Pew) using the internet has increased from just below 40 per cent in 1998 to 75 per cent in December 2007. That is a staggering increase of nearly 87.5 per cent in the number of users in only nine years! Interestingly, results from one of Pew's recently conducted tracking surveys (October–December 2007) indicate that adults in every age range are online (ibid.). Broken down by age group, we see that there are still more younger users, but the number of mature (Pew's term) users is not insignificant (Table 2.1). Note that these percentages are based on the 75 per cent of adults using the internet, as reported by Pew. These numbers are significant, especially when we begin looking at how youth are currently using the internet as well.

The Urban Libraries Council (ULC) teamed up with the School of Informatics at the State University of New York at Buffalo and conducted a study to determine how youth's use

**Table 2.1** **Demographics of internet users, October–December 2007**

| Age | Percentage |
|---|---|
| 18–29 | 92 |
| 30–49 | 85 |
| 50–64 | 72 |
| 65+ | 37 |

*Source*: Pew Internet & American Life Project (2008)

of the internet complements and/or impacts their use of public libraries. *The Impacts of the Internet on Public Library Use* goes into detailed analysis of the results (Urban Libraries Council, 2004). For our purposes, however, the study yielded two significant findings:

- 100 per cent of the youth reported that they had access to the internet from one or more locations;
- the most frequently used source of internet access was at home (73.3 per cent).

Youth are, as illustrated and as expected, far more likely to seek information from home than from the physical library. Take this evidence coupled with Pew's, and the implications are clear: more and more youth and adults alike are using the internet to communicate and/or gather information.

## *To personalize the internet experience*

There are those in the reference community who oppose virtual reference based on the belief that it is an impersonal method of delivery for a service that should be personal. They further believe that providing reference virtually risks offending patrons, as body language is not part of the online equation. Our point here is not to involve ourselves in this debate, but to frame our belief that virtual reference personalizes the internet experience.

As we hear more and more about 'information overload' and as librarians lament our patrons' inability to separate the wheat from the chaff online, virtual reference gives us an opportunity to insert our services into our users' online experiences. Coffman (2003: 7) finds it ironic 'that at a time when our traditional reference services are languishing from want of use, many people need exactly the kind of personal assistance we have always offered in finding what they are looking for on the web'. We agree! Librarians providing virtual reference add a personal dimension to virtual research, just as librarians providing traditional reference add a personal dimension to traditional research.

## *To reach patrons who might not otherwise be reachable*

An increasing number of students are opting to pursue college education online via distance learning programs. And demographics indicate that this trend is growing and will continue to do so. According to the most recent statistics available, the number of students enrolled in distance education courses nearly doubled from about 1.6 million in 1997–1998 to nearly 3.1 million during the 2000–2001 academic year (US Department of Education, 1999, 2003). Another staggering increase in a few short years! These distance students are already online, and virtual reference is, for them, a powerful option as it provides access to person-to-person reference and also brings them a bit more into the loop of their respective universities.

Deaf and hearing-impaired people are another group that stand to benefit from virtual reference services. Peters and

Bell (2006) explain past technological advances in library service provision to the deaf and hearing-impaired, and deem instant messaging to be an effective and practical way to reach this user segment because it is text-based and also since librarians use this technology often enough that they won't forget how to use it, as has happened in the past.

Shy people and housebound people are also population groups that might appreciate the opportunities virtual reference provides. Indeed, even those who are reachable – teens, heavy computer users – would likely welcome another avenue of access!

## *To maintain a competitive edge in the information arena*

Much of the literature these days encourages and warns librarians that to keep ourselves afloat, we must continue to demonstrate that our services are useful and needed. Especially needed. We know that librarians provide valuable service; the onus is on us to make sure our patrons know this too, and further to be where they can find and may expect to find us.

Mon (2006), Lipow (2003) and Coffman and Arret (2004a, 2004b) all discuss why libraries should, and how they can, maintain a competitive edge in the information arena.

## *To provide, and continue providing, quality service*

The shift from library as warehouse to library as information utility reminds us that our focus first must be on providing informed and informative reference services to our patrons.

Building a collection (warehouse) remains integral, of course, but not in the forefront as it once was (Greer and Grover, 1995).

Convenience factors into quality service. RUSA, by way of introduction to its *Guidelines for Implementing and Maintaining Virtual Reference Services*, acknowledges that library resources are increasingly virtual, and therefore reference services should be too: 'Technology now allows users to submit their queries to the library at any time from any place in the world. Virtual reference is responsive to patrons' need for convenient access to reference service' (American Library Association, 2004). And so, to reach their audience, reference librarians need to be where that audience is, and a sizeable portion are online!

One more item of note in this section: virtual reference provides transcripts of reference transactions. This is significant, since it allows librarians to analyze those transactions and determine methods to improve reference service.

## Is virtual reference perfect?

No, of course not. E-mail is asynchronous and could require multiple communications until the reference request is completely understood. Chat and IM involve software downloads which could be problematic. Also, much of the software was developed for one-on-one conversations, not for services that might answer a high volume of questions (Coffman, 2003: 1–18). And, as widely discussed, privacy and security are worrisome to the library community – see Chapter 9 for more on privacy and security.

## Basic models for virtual reference: e-mail, web-based chat and instant messaging

E-mail, web-based chat and IM are the three major delivery vehicles for virtual reference. They need not be mutually exclusive; indeed, they complement each other well in certain scenarios. Our purpose here is to touch briefly upon features of the three main delivery methods for virtual reference (Table 2.2). We hope that by comparing IM to so-called web-based chat and e-mail, you'll have a greater understanding of IM's context in the broader world of virtual reference. Remember, too, that other technologies, such as voice over IP and videoconferencing, aren't even mentioned here. The world of virtual reference is vast! IM is just a sliver of that world.

### *Synchronous?*

Synchronous services are delivered in real time with no delay. Both web-based chat and IM are synchronous; e-mail is not. Synchronous is not, by definition, preferred to or superior to asynchronous virtual reference. It is simply different.

### *Software download required?*

Many cite the need to download software to use virtual reference services as a disadvantage. We would argue that while for a few it might be an obstacle, for most it would not, given the demographics of internet users today. (Here we do make the assumption that internet users are our target patron segment, since those who do not use or are uncomfortable

**Table 2.2** Virtual reference models at a glance

| | E-mail | Web-based chat | IM |
|---|---|---|---|
| **Synchronous?** | No | Yes | Yes |
| **Software download required?** | No | Sometimes | Sometimes |
| **User familiar with technology?** | Generally high | Varies; most users unfamiliar with library-specific chat programs | Varies; younger users more consistently familiar |
| **Librarian familiar with technology?** | High | Varies | Varies |
| **Technical requirements for library** | Existing | Varies | Minimal |
| **If librarian is busy?** | Libraries often indicate a wait time of 24–48 hours for a response | Varies<br>Typically routes to another librarian if one is available | Typical IM set-up allows no routing of chats<br>If librarian is busy, patron waits; this is changing with new collaborative IM software such as LibraryH3lp |
| **Additional staff needed?** | Rarely | Depends on traffic | Depends on traffic |
| **Page pushing?** | No | Available, but depends on product | No |
| **Co-browsing?** | No | Available, but depends on product | No |
| **Security and privacy?** | Somewhat secure<br>Not private | Varies, but can be robust | Somewhat secure<br>Not private |
| **Cost?** | Inexpensive | Large range, depending on product<br>Can be quite expensive | Inexpensive |

with the internet will come into the physical library.) A large percentage of library patrons already have e-mail accounts and/or IM. In the early days of web-based chat, it was often necessary for patrons to download software to their computers in order to participate in a chat with a librarian. This is rarely the case with these products any more. Additionally, with the use of 'widgets' it is possible to put an IM chatbox on your website, allowing patrons who do not themselves use IM to chat with you via IM.

### User familiar with technology?

Again, assuming a computer-literate patron base, users will be quite familiar with both e-mail and IM services. Web-based chat might not be as familiar, but most programs are user-friendly enough so as not to pose an obstacle.

### Librarian familiar with technology?

We can safely assume that most or all librarians are skilled e-mail users. As for web-based chat and IM, while many librarians are comfortable using these virtual communication methods, many remain unfamiliar with their use. As we'll discuss in future chapters, IM software is typically extraordinarily easy to use! Because web-based chat software tends to be much more fully featured than IM software, it has a steeper learning curve for librarians.

### Technical requirements for the library?

None of the methods for providing virtual reference (e-mail, web-based chat or IM) necessarily requires any special technological set-up in your library. E-mail and IM both use standard, lightweight consumer software. Web-based chat services are typically hosted off-site by the provider of the software and service. Some chat software can be hosted in-house, in which case the library will need to have a server and the skills to maintain it. IM and chat both require fast access to the internet.

### *If librarian is busy?*

Since e-mail is asynchronous, whether the librarian is currently assisting another patron is not an issue. With web-based chat, depending on the software, users may be placed in a queue. With IM, this is more problematic. Because IM software was really designed for an individual end-user doing one-on-one chats, the idea of more than one computer workstation monitoring the same IM account is a fairly new one. 'Out of the box' IM really provides no mechanisms for coping with a busy reference desk, no easy way to transfer chats to a back-up librarian, etc. That said, exciting work is being done in the area of collaborative IM, with new services appearing that make such routing and queuing possible! For more details, check out Chapter 8.

### *Additional staff needed?*

E-mail is still a viable virtual reference option, but in most cases the traffic will not be so overwhelming as to necessitate additional staffing, as the standard and expected wait time for an e-mail response is 24–48 hours. For synchronous web-based chat and IM, the answer is that it depends. It depends on the traditional reference desk traffic, the virtual reference traffic and on librarians' comfort with multitasking. To provide the quality service we would like, patrons should not have to wait too long either face to face or online. It follows logically that if either the traditional or the virtual reference desk is too busy to be responsive enough, additional staff should be considered.

## Page pushing and co-browsing?

Page pushing and co-browsing are standard features in most virtual reference software. They offer the ability to replicate the 'guiding' activities that are so essential to the face-to-face reference interview. The OCLC defines co-browsing as 'Joint use, by a librarian and a patron in different locations, of a Web browser to access Web pages, databases, forms and records, with shared mouse and keyboard control. Lets the librarian and the patron navigate the Web together remotely, viewing the same Web pages and databases' (OCLC QuestionPoint glossary). The OCLC defines page pushing as the 'Automatic display of a Web page on a patron's computer screen by sending the page's URL to the patron during a chat session' (ibid.). Generally speaking, these are features we will not find when using 'out of the box' commercial IM software to provide IM reference services. Instant messaging software is designed with a general consumer end-user in mind; it is not tailored to the services we provide. That said, there are plug-ins (e.g. the WebEx plug-in for Yahoo! Messenger) that can provide co-browsing capabilities. Enterprise IM software also provides co-browsing functionality. We will discuss plug-ins and enterprise IM extensively in later chapters.

Page pushing and co-browsing are, obviously, not available in e-mail reference services.

## Security and privacy?

We discuss IM security issues in depth in Chapter 9. In brief, users of IM software face similar security and privacy issues as users of e-mail: unencrypted communications and vulnerability to viruses and worms because files can be transferred. Web-based chat software varies in terms of encryption, but most offers encrypted sessions.

### *Cost?*

E-mail reference can be conducted without spending any money on software. IM software is almost always available as a free download. Some companies offer premium versions of their software for a fee; for example, Cerulean Studios' Trillian software is free for the basic download and $25 for the 'professional' version. Web-based chat services, however, do have higher costs associated with them: these vary depending on the product, the number of users, the number of special features enabled, etc. Costs will often include a set-up fee in addition to an annual license and/or charge per 'seat' (user). Jody Condit Fagan (2005) reported set-up fees in the $1,000 range, and annual license fees around $2,000–3,000. These figures are offered to give you a sense of the relative costs of the various methods of providing virtual reference.

## Summary

In this chapter we introduced virtual reference via RUSA's comprehensive definition. We looked, briefly, at how virtual reference got its start, with the IPL as a pioneer and primary example. We believe, as you know because we have written this book, that there are many reasons to consider providing virtual reference and we talked about some of them. Why not? Patrons of all ages are increasingly on the internet. Virtual reference can personalize the internet experience;

reach patrons who might not otherwise be reachable; maintain a competitive edge in the information arena; and provide, and continue providing, quality service. We have rounded out the chapter with a table summarizing features of the three main modes of delivering virtual reference – e-mail, web-based chat and IM.

Now that we have our background, let's dig in and learn about IM!

3

# IM basics

## What is instant messaging?

Instant messaging has come to mean rather a lot of things in the last few years but, at its most basic, IM is an internet service that allows users to communicate with one another directly in real time. The concept of presence awareness lies at the very heart of IM. That is, when users sign in to their IM account, they are able to see which of their contacts are online and available for instant messaging.

Although this book will focus almost exclusively on text chats, IM networks can be used to share all manner of material, not just text. This includes video, sound, streaming content, web links and images. In this chapter we hope to give you the lay of the land: why instant messaging is timely technology, an overview of the history of instant messaging, a summary of how it works and a sense of the software that's out there for you to use.

## Why IM?

IM is currently used among all age groups to varying degrees, and usage continues increasing across the board. The Pew Internet & American Life Project's 'How Americans use instant messaging' report (Shiu and Lenhart, 2004) comprehensively explores IM use among internet users, reporting that 53 million Americans use IM. Salient findings from the report that librarians considering an IM reference service should be aware of include the following.

- Although most internet users favor e-mail over IM as a form of communication, nearly a quarter of IM users say they instant message more than they e-mail.
- A majority of IM users say they do other things on their computer and online at the same time they are participating in IM sessions.
- Fifteen per cent of IM users say they use a wireless device such as a phone or wireless laptop to send and receive IM messages.
- Twenty-four per cent of IM users say they have IMed a person who was in the same location as they were.

Note that these statistics were gathered from Pew's May–June 2004 tracking surveys. As this is Pew's most recent comprehensive IM report, we can safely assume higher percentages as all other indicators point to increasing IM usage. In brief, IM use is up and IM is becoming a more pervasive technology.

## IM: a very brief history

Pretty much as long as people have been connecting computers to networks they have been using those computers to engage in person-to-person communication over those networks. Whether using early peer-to-peer communication protocols like 'talk' or protocols that required users to log in to a server like IRC (Internet Relay Chat), there were ways for early users of the internet to chat with one another. As the popularity of the internet increased, online services like America Online (AOL), CompuServe and Prodigy began offering users chatrooms and other communication tools. Instant messaging as we know it today, though, really began in 1996 with the introduction of ICQ.

ICQ, which is meant as a kind of shorthand for 'I seek you', was developed by the Israeli company Mirablis. Unlike the chat services offered by the major online providers like AOL and CompuServe, ICQ was a piece of software users installed on their computers (a 'client'). This software would then communicate with the ICQ servers and let users know when their contacts were online. ICQ used its own proprietary protocol for sending and receiving information. Both participants in a conversation needed to have accounts on the service in order to chat with one another. This basic model is how IM works today. We'll examine the details of the model more closely in the next section.

## How does it work?

The basic model developed by Mirablis for its ICQ product in 1996 remains the dominant model for IM services. The basic steps in the model are getting started, launching the client and getting connected and chatting.

### *Getting started*

The user goes to the website for the IM service they want to use (e.g. AOL, Yahoo!, MSN, ICQ, etc.).

The user creates an account for that service.

The user downloads and installs a piece of client software on their personal computer. Typically, this is the software developed by the IM service (e.g. AOL Instant Messenger, Yahoo! Messenger, etc.). We will talk about clients that support multiple services in a bit; let's keep it simple for now. There are many options for users who wish to use IM solely on the web without downloading and installing IM software. Again, we'll discuss those later.

## Launching the client and getting connected

The user launches the software ('the client'), signing in with the user name and password she acquired during account set-up.

The client will connect with the IM service's server via a proprietary protocol.

The client sends the server the IP address of the computer you're using and the port number assigned to the IM client. At the same time, it will send a list of all of the user's 'contacts' (or 'buddies') to the server. If this is the first time the user has signed in, they obviously won't have any contacts yet.

The service checks to see if any of the people on the user's contact list are currently signed in.

If the service finds any of the user's contacts online, it will send the user's connection information (IP and port) to the contact's client. The user's status on the contact's buddy list will change from offline to online. The contact's information will also be sent to the user (Figure 3.1).

## Chatting

The user clicks the name on her 'contact list' or 'buddy list' of the contact with whom she wishes to chat. A window pops open into which the user can type her message. After the message has been typed, the user clicks 'Send'.

This message is sent directly to the contact's computer, it does not go through the IM service's server (Figure 3.2). This is possible because the connection information

**Figure 3.1** How IM works: client computers communicating with central IM server

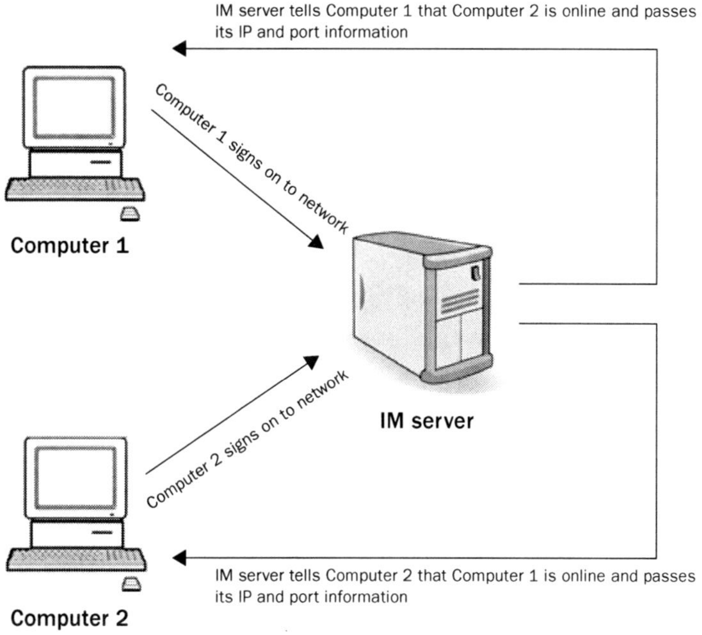


**Figure 3.2** How IM works: client computers communicating directly

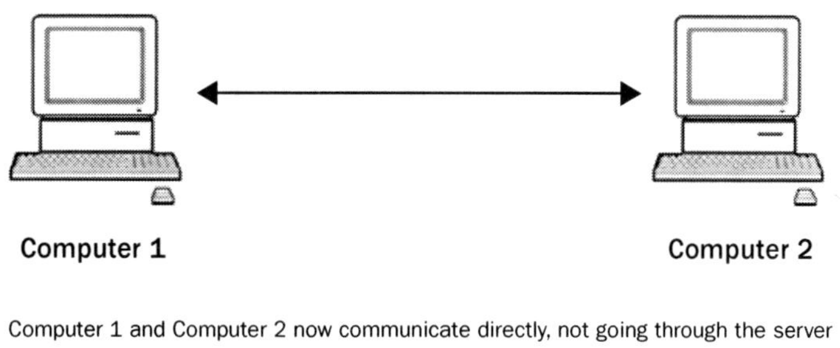


was 'swapped' when the user connected to the service. A window with the user's message will pop up on the contact's screen.

# Protocols and clients

## *Protocols/networks*

The basic model for IM service is based on IM service providers using their own propriety protocols for communication. For users, this lack of standards has meant that they can only communicate with others on the same network. If Jane is an AOL IM user and Pete is a Yahoo! IM user, they will not be able to chat. Pete will have to create an account on AOL in order to chat with Jane. Compare this with e-mail, where the use of shared standards allows users of one e-mail provider to exchange e-mail with the users of any other provider.

In 1999 an open, standard protocol named Jabber (now known as XMPP) was launched to try to address this problem. We'll talk more about XMPP later in the book (see Chapter 8), but we'll keep it simple for now. XMPP is designed to work more like e-mail – anyone can set up a server and each user has a unique address. This move towards open standards is incredibly important; unfortunately, all this talk of protocols and standards can be pretty intimidating or distracting for the librarian who just wants to get started with a simple IM reference service!

There are a lot of IM networks out there, many of which are quite niche or obscure. For the purposes of this book, we're mostly talking about the four 'biggies', but we'll touch on some others as well. Table 3.1 describes briefly the four protocols that are most commonly used and that you'll want to consider using with your IM service.

## *Clients*

One thing that can be confusing when you're getting started with IM is how tightly coupled the *service provider* and the

**Table 3.1 Major IM protocols**

| Protocol | Year released | Open/proprietary |
|---|---|---|
| Oscar (AOL and ICQ) | 1997 | Proprietary |
| YMSG (Yahoo!) | 1998 | Proprietary |
| MSNP (Microsoft) | 1999 | Proprietary |
| XMPP (Jabber) | 1999 | Open |

*client* can be. For instance, if you have an account on AOL to use its instant messaging service, you are likely also using the AOL instant messaging software client to connect to that service. But you don't have to!

If we again compare this with e-mail, we can think of it this way. You might get your e-mail service from, for instance, your workplace or your phone company. You can then choose to use any of number of software programs to access your e-mail. You might use Thunderbird or Outlook to access the same account. In some cases, you might access your e-mail through software provided by the company that provides the e-mail service – like with Hotmail or Gmail.

It's important to keep this distinction between your IM accounts and the software you use to access them clear in your mind. This can all get very convoluted, especially once we start talking about adding chat widgets on to your website!

There was a time when if you wanted to be signed in and available on multiple IM services (because you had friends/colleagues on various networks), you had to install and run software for each of the services. This was because there was no software that supported multiple IM services. That has all changed, though. Now there are a number of clients which allow you to connect to multiple services through a single client. We'll talk more about how that works in the next chapter.

## *Components of the IM client*

### The contact list

Earlier we described 'presence awareness' as the heart of IM, and the 'buddy' or 'contact' list is where we really see that in action. The contact list, unsurprisingly, lists your contacts. That is, it provides you with a list of all of the other users of that system who you've identified as contacts and gives you information about their status. You can see if a friend or colleague is currently online and available to chat, online but busy with something else or offline. The contact list, as described above, is also the interface for initiating an IM conversation. You click on a contact's name in order to start a conversation with her.

Figure 3.3 is a picture of Rachel's 'contact list' in Adium. Each of her online contacts is listed: the icons next to the contacts' names are either green, indicating that the contact is online and available, or red, indicating that the person is away or busy. Her contacts can, optionally, set a status message to explain their status. In the example, several contacts have included status messages. Rachel has configured her contact list to show only those contacts who are currently signed into their accounts.

### Account information and preferences

Whichever client you choose to use, there will be a way to set up your account information. This is where you type in your screen name and password and set any preferences you have (Figure 3.4). We'll talk about this more in Chapter 4, when we discuss how to set up your accounts.

### The chat window

The chat window is where you will conduct your IM conversations. Chat windows vary depending on the client

**Figure 3.3** Example of an IM contact or 'buddy' list

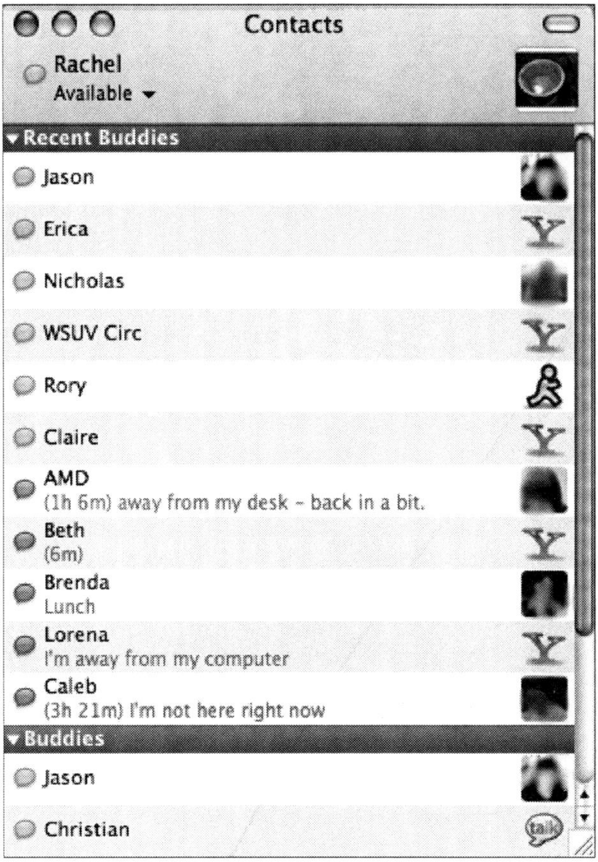


you decide to use, but the basic interface is very simple – a box to type in and a box to read the conversation in. Clicking on a name will pop open a chat window. In this software, you type in the box and then hit 'return' to send your message. In Figure 3.5, Rachel clicked on Claire's name and typed her message into the box. When she hits 'return', the message she typed will move into the top part of the chat window. Claire's response, when it comes, will appear in the top part of the window after Rachel's (Figure 3.6).

**Figure 3.4** Entering your account information into the IM client

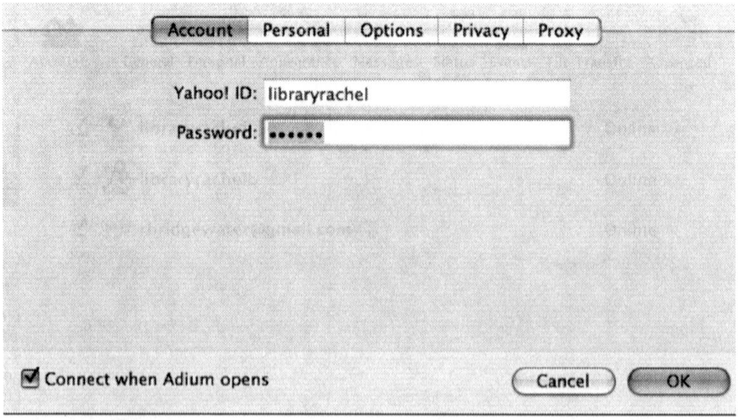


**Figure 3.5** Example of an IM chat window

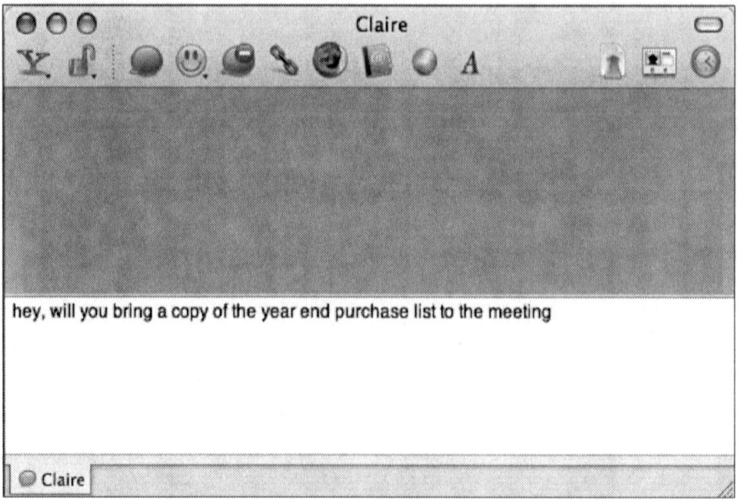


Looking across the top of the chat window you can see that, in Adium, options for working with your chat are provided at the top of the window. To give you a sense of the kinds of features available in IM, we'll review some of the depicted icons here.

**Figure 3.6** Example of a chat in progress

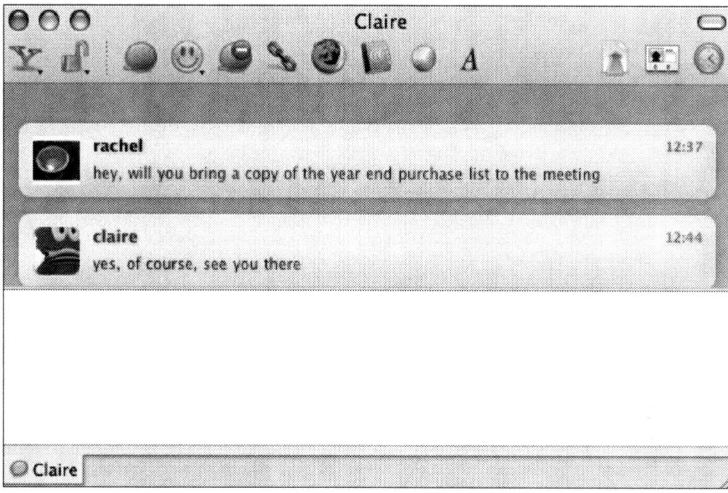


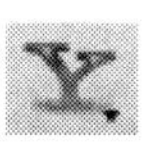 This first icon indicates that Rachel is chatting with Claire using her Yahoo! account (because Claire is chatting via Yahoo!). Adium allows Rachel to access all of her accounts at once.

 Adium allows encrypted chat using OTR (see Chapter 9 for more details on encryption). This lock lets Rachel know whether she's having a private chat or an unencrypted chat.

 This smiley face allows the user to select from a list of 'emoticons'. People differ in their feelings about emoticons, but we believe that they do help convey some non-verbal content that is difficult to get across otherwise. We'd recommend sparing use of emoticons. Figure 3.7 gives a sense of the array of emoticons available (in Adium they differ slightly depending on which client you are using).

 This icon allows Rachel to 'block' someone who is chatting with her. When someone has been blocked he will

**Figure 3.7** **Emoticons**

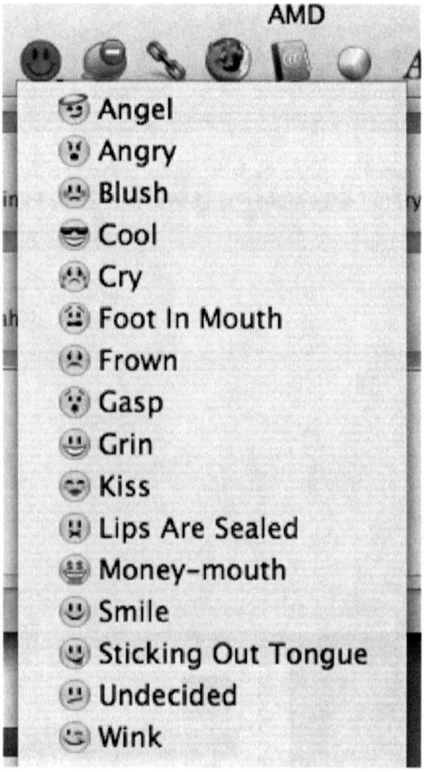


no longer be able to see your status or contact you. Naturally, in a library setting we would want to use this button sparingly. However, if you have ongoing problems with spam or harassment, it is useful to know that blocking a contact is an option.

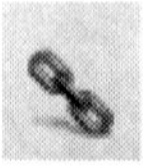 This inserts a hyperlink. This can be a nice way to insert a link as you can specify text instead of a long, ugly URL (see Figure 3.8). The inserted URL will, in theory, look to the recipient as shown in Figure 3.9.

It is important to keep in mind, though, that fancy tricks which work nicely in one client might not translate to

**Figure 3.8** Inserting a link into a chat

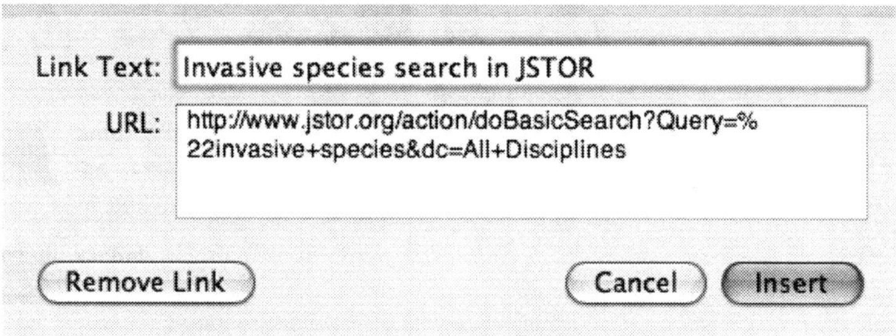


**Figure 3.9** URL inserted into a chat, formatted successfully

another client. In Figures 3.8 and 3.9 we've just shown Rachel's side of the conversation. Figure 3.10 shows what Claire's side looks like in Meebo, a web-based client. It looks fine and gets the job done, but the nicely formatted URL didn't 'translate'.

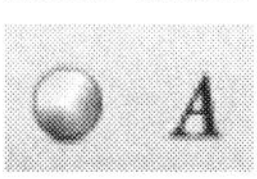

These two icons allow you to format your chat. Most basic formatting like font size and style (bold, italics, etc.) will translate across most clients.

This opens up a dialog to send files over IM.

This is a brief tour through some of the chat features that are part of Adium. You could expect to find similar, but not

**Figure 3.10** **Using the link dialog doesn't guarantee results in all clients**

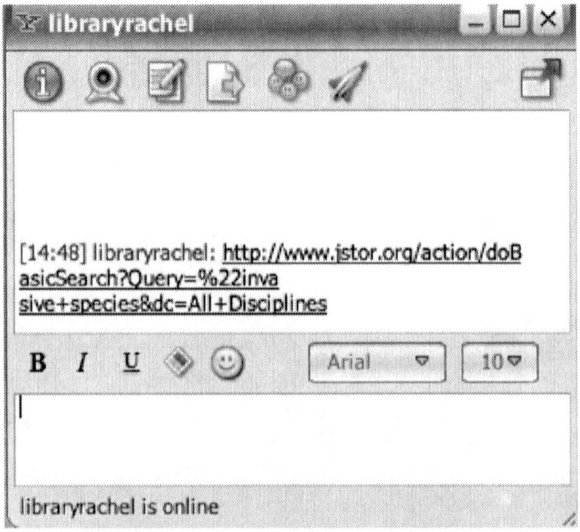


identical, features in other clients. Looking at the Meebo chat window in Figure 3.10, you can see that some of the same features are there but look different. An important thing to keep in mind about IM is that the basic 'window to read in, window to type in' features are all you really need to know about in order to chat effectively. The rest of the features are just, as they say, gravy.

## Presence indicators and status messages

Just as you can see your contacts' status when you look at them on your contact list, you can set statuses for yourself in your client. By default, you'll show up as 'Available' when you're online and 'Away' if you set your client to Away, or you set your preferences to show you as 'Away' after a period of inactivity (Figure 3.11). It is also possible to set and save custom 'Away' messages. More on this in Chapter 4.

**Figure 3.11** Status messages

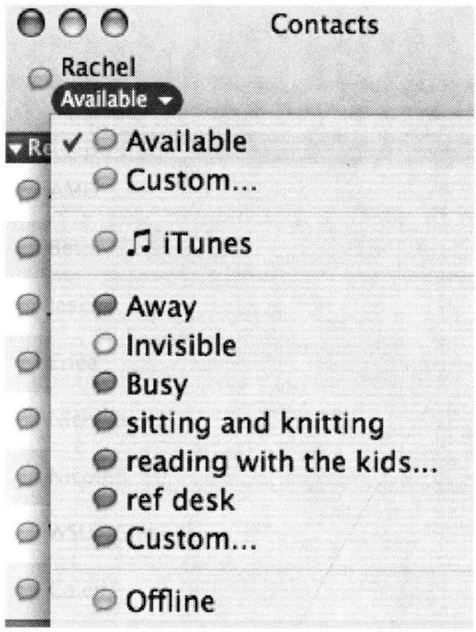


## *What? No chart?!*

In drafting this book we were sure we'd want to include a chart of all of the major IM clients and their features. The truth is, though, that this information changes much too quickly for a book! In the time we've been writing, massive changes have taken place in the world of IM clients and we know that these changes will continue. At the time of writing, Wikipedia has a marvelous chart of IM clients and their features that is being regularly maintained. As with all things Wikipedia, that may change, but it was certainly the best source we found for comparing the features of different IM clients.

So we won't be providing a big chart full of IM clients and their features, but we will meet you halfway and provide

**Table 3.2** **IM clients**

| Clients for IM reference: a snapshot |
|---|
| *Pidgin*. An open source multi-protocol IM client. Pidgin runs on Windows and Linux. |
| *Adium*. An open source multi-protocol IM client based on Pidgin. Adium is Mac only. |
| *Trillian and Trillian Pro*. A proprietary multi-protocol IM client. Trillian is Windows only as of this writing. Trillian is free; Trillian Pro can be purchased and includes more features than the free version. |
| *Meebo and other web-based clients*. Increasingly, libraries are discovering and using web-only clients like Meebo. This area of the IM world is changing fast! |

a kind of snapshot of IM clients typically/successfully used for IM reference as of this writing (Table 3.2).

## Summary

You really do not need to be in any way technically inclined to understand all you need to know to operate a successful IM reference service. If you can keep straight the idea that there are multiple proprietary protocols for IM service (like AOL and Yahoo!), and that users of one protocol can only talk to users of that same protocol, you'll be in good shape. Next, remember that the software you use to access your accounts on one of these services can (and probably should!) be un-coupled from the service provider. In other words, you don't have to use AOL's instant messaging software in order to use your AOL account. You can, instead, use a multi-protocol software that will allow you to sign into all of your accounts at once. If you understand these basic concepts, you'll be able to get your IM reference service up and running in no time!

4

# Basic IM reference – set-up and use

What does it take to get an IM reference service up and running? Erica Carlson Nicol from Washington State University in Pullman, WA, describes the experience of one large, land-grant university:

> Several factors have gone into making an instant messaging reference service at the WSU Libraries in Pullman possible: the increased availability and quality of freely available, multi-platform IM clients, library employees' growing awareness of the possibilities of IM, and the employees' willingness to experiment and play with a new (to most of them) vehicle for reference services. Several of us had experience working with Gaim (now Pidgin) and found it to be a useful IM client, and many of the library employees at the WSU Libraries in Pullman could see that IM reference service would be a part of our future. In addition to watching our patrons use instant messaging, and hearing about IM reference with increasing frequency at library conferences, list-serv discussions, and conversations with fellow library workers, our colleagues at WSU Vancouver had already successfully begun IM reference.

On 23 February Lorena O'English presented a learning break to interested WSU Libraries employees about the possibilities of IM reference services using Meebo, a multi-platform, web-based IM client. The learning break inspired me to send an e-mail message out to a small group of WSU Pullman colleagues:

> The combination of Online Northwest and Lorena's IM presentation have started me thinking of ways that we can start getting some more widespread acceptance of IM (with an eye towards reference). I think it might be helpful to start a kind of 'early adopter' group who could use IM to communicate with each other, and this group seemed as good a test bed as anyone could ask for. Anyone want to try using IM for the next couple of weeks and see how it goes? If you want in, feel free to respond through e-mail or to IM me. I'm going to have either Gaim or Meebo running daily for a while in an attempt to get into a good IM-ing habit.

This led to a good deal of instant messaging among willing librarians, mostly using Meebo, and led to a cohort of library employees who knew the ins and outs of instant messaging before it became a formal way of offering reference services.

In March 2007 the libraries made the decision to begin IM reference services, starting at the end of the spring semester and allowing employees the chance to familiarize themselves with IM during the slower summer months. The existing level of familiarity with Meebo among library employees, as well as the client's simple interface and the ease with which Meebo widgets can be created, were all factors in the selection of Meebo as the client used by the WSU Pullman Libraries.

## Preparations

An intentionally laid-back approach was taken to the implementation of IM reference, partly to emphasize the ease and informality of instant messaging, and partly to avoid anxieties of the sort that had resulted in an earlier attempt of the WSU Libraries to provide 24/7 virtual reference services. Beth Lindsay, head of public services and outreach, set up Meebo accounts for the Owen Science Library and for the Holland and Terrell Libraries, and provided training sessions on IM reference for librarians. The training sessions introduced some basic IM concepts and also provided an opportunity for many librarians to see Meebo's interface for the first time.

The librarians in the Holland and Terrell Libraries put together a week of 'practice' IM sessions in April, where volunteers sent messages to librarians and information assistants working at the reference desk. Feedback from this practice week was very valuable. The two biggest lessons learned were that the computer hardware at the reference desk was insufficient to support IM and that training was needed for librarians and information assistants who were unfamiliar with instant messaging.

The two computers at the reference desk in the Holland and Terrell Libraries were set up to prohibit sound. During the practice week, instant message queries that were sent while reference workers were busy on other webpages were often left to languish, not catching the reference workers' attention until too late. New computer monitors that enabled sound proved to be a great help in increasing the number of IM questions that were answered quickly.

Feedback from participants in the IM practice week also highlighted the need for more training for reference desk workers who weren't used to instant messaging. While Meebo's interface appeared intuitive to many library employees, it was not intuitive to all of them. Web-based instant messaging was a new concept to many, and, after some tries at using IM, there were also many questions about IM procedures at a reference desk that was very often busy with in-person patrons. Adding to the need for training was the fact that Meebo, being a relatively new client designed for an audience that is comfortable with trial and error, has a very brief help page that didn't answer most of the questions that our reference workers have.

I worked to create a training PowerPoint that gives an overview of Meebo's features, provides some trouble-shooting information and discusses instant messaging procedures at the reference desk. I am currently working with Steve Borrelli to create a flash tutorial from this information to provide to librarians and information assistants who are new to the reference desk or who want refreshing on how to use Meebo. More open discussion was also created so that the people who worked with IM at the reference desk knew who they could contact with questions.

### Publicity

There was very little publicity for our IM services when they first became live. Our IM publicity team decided that it would be best to advertise the service as the 2007 fall semester starts. We expect to have announcements out and posters up to announce our new IM services as our students and faculty arrive at the beginning of another academic year.

A webpage that describes our IM services was created by Mark O'English and brought live in May 2007. It can be found at www.wsulibs.wsu.edu/24-7/IM.html. The page includes Meebo widgets that patrons can use to send instant message questions to the Owen Science and Holland and Terrell reference librarians. The page also includes links to the libraries' privacy policy and to the privacy policies of commonly used IM clients, such as Yahoo!, MSN, Google Talk, and, of course, to Meebo's privacy policy.

### Going live

IM reference services went live in late April 2007. Some adjustment on the part of reference desk workers took place as the new service became available to the public. IM reference is currently offered by the employees who staff the reference desks, who log into the library IM accounts as their shifts begin. For now that means that our IM reference services are offered during the same hours as our in-person reference services.

As IM is a fairly new service for us, reference librarians and information assistants are still learning how to work gracefully with IM patrons at reference desks that are frequently active. We learned to create 'I'm helping another patron' status messages so that IM patrons wouldn't feel ignored if their queries weren't answered immediately, and we learned how easy it is to forget to change our IM status messages, and to forget to log into Meebo when we started our reference shifts. We prioritize the patrons who stand in front of us, asking for help, but are learning to say, 'Let me finish up with this IM reference question', when patrons find us typing information into Meebo when they come to the desk.

> Currently we don't keep separate statistics for IM questions, so they show up as regular reference or directional questions. However, we are probably averaging two to three IM queries per week, and expect the number of queries to pick up as the fall semester starts and as we publicize the service. (Erica Carlson Nicol, Washington State University Pullman)

We imagine you were probably sold on the idea of instant messaging reference before you even picked up this book, and are ready to jump in and get your service started. There are things you need to do with people right away (talk about training, staffing, policies, etc.) and things you need to do with computers right away (set up accounts and download software). These two classes of activities interact with one another – a decision you make about staffing will affect choices you make about software, for instance – but we're going to take each separately for now.

## Choosing services

As discussed in Chapter 3, you will need to create accounts for each of the services you intend to use. We strongly suggest that you create accounts on *at least* the most popular services like AOL, Yahoo! and MSN. Remember, you can always add more accounts as you need/want them.

## Choosing screen names

Put some thought into choosing screen names for your library reference service, but not so much thought that it paralyzes you. Endeavor to register the same screen name for each of the services you use (when possible). This will make things easier for everyone! Pick a name that is meaningful, easy to remember and flexible enough to grow with your service. When we set up our IM service at Washington State University in Vancouver we chose 'wsuvlibrary'. Our colleagues at the much larger Washington State University campus in Pullman, Washington, set up screen names for the humanities and social science library, Holland, and other names for the science library, Owen. They use 'hollandwsuref' and 'owenwsuref'. Oberlin College Libraries use 'ObieRef'. At Yale University they chose 'yalelib'. These are all just examples of effective screen names that make sense in the communities they serve.

Signing up for a screen name is easy. Visit the website for the service you'd like to use and follow the sign-up process. Repeat for each service that you'd like to create an account on.

To illustrate this process, we've used some screen captures from the Yahoo! Messenger website. Keep in mind that the specifics of what we'll show you here will vary from service to service and, indeed, by the time you read this it's likely the Yahoo! site will look different.

Visit the website for the IM service you'd like to use. Note that, quite often, the first page will encourage you to download the IM client associated with that service (Figure 4.1). You may want to do that, but more likely you'll want to use one of the multi-protocol services available. Scan the page for a 'sign-up' link or click on the 'download' link – the sign-up link is probably lurking on the next page (Figure 4.2). Once you've located it, click on the 'sign-up' link.

Fill in the form (Figure 4.3), choose a screen name and you're ready to go! Remember, or jot down, your screen name (in the example, your screen name is your Yahoo! ID) and password. You'll need them when you set up your software.

**Figure 4.1** Yahoo! Messenger website

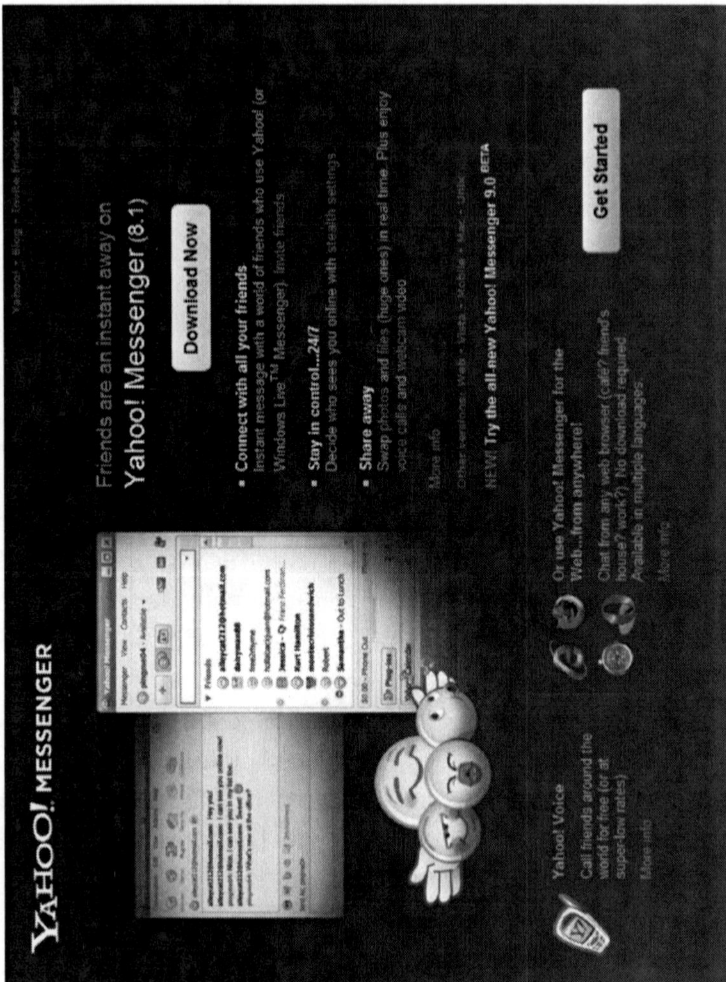

**Figure 4.2** Yahoo! Messenger site with sign-up link

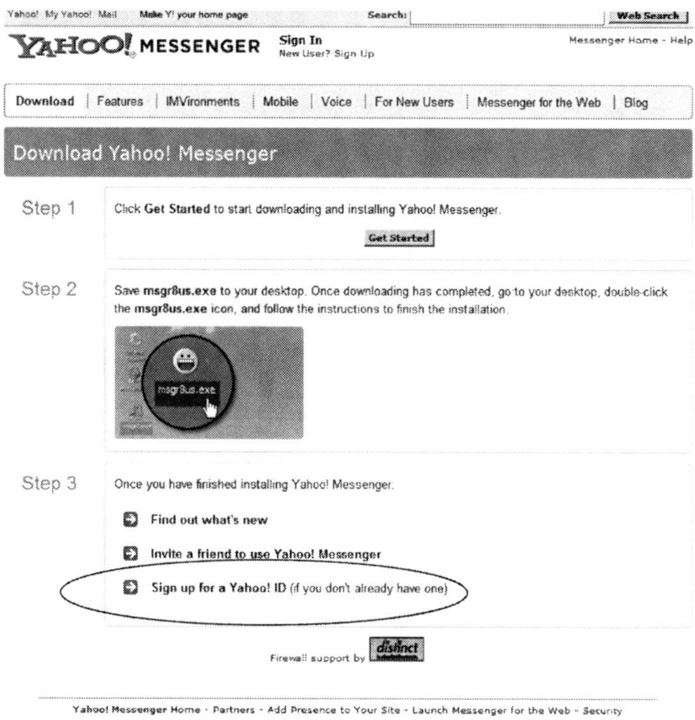


## Choosing a client

In Chapter 3 we discussed the 'anatomy' of an IM client. When choosing an IM client, you'll want to look at the features it offers, how it looks and how it handles common tasks. Don't hesitate to download a few and play around with them to see what you like. Some features or qualities of an IM client will be 'deal breakers' – for instance, you'll need a client that works on the operating system you use. Other features will be less important and come down to pure personal preference. Below we review some of the things you should look for:

**Figure 4.3** Signing up for a Yahoo! Messenger account

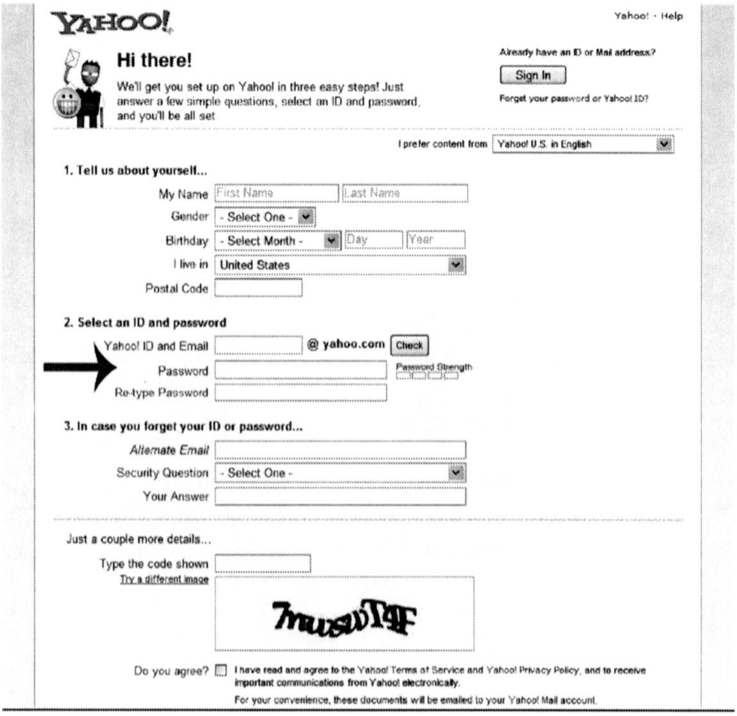


- multi-protocol versus single protocol;
- web-based versus PC-based;
- features;
- open source versus proprietary;
- operating system;
- cost/advertisements;
- encryption options.

Ultimately, most clients work basically the same way. Find a client that runs on your operating system, that supports multiple protocols and that you find pleasing to use, and you'll be okay!

## Multi-protocol versus single protocol

Will you be able to serve the majority of your patrons using a single piece of client software? Look for a client that supports all the major protocols used by your user population. If you don't know which services your population uses, it's a safe bet that you'll be well covered if your client supports AIM (the Oscar protocol), Yahoo!, MSN and Jabber. As of this writing the major multi-protocol clients are Pidgin (open source – Windows and Unix), Trillian (proprietary – Windows only), Adium (open source – Mac only) and Meebo (proprietary – web-based).

## Web-based versus PC-based

Until fairly recently, if you wanted to IM you had to install software in order to do it. There are exceptions to this – most of the major IM providers have some web-based version of their clients – but, for the most part, IM meant software installed on your computer. For the last few years, though, web-based IM clients have been growing in popularity. Meebo is the best known of these at the time of writing, and is an excellent example of this class of IM clients.

The user goes to the Meebo website (Figure 4.4) and can sign on to any or all of the networks listed there. Users also have the option of creating a Meebo ID and signing into Meebo only once, having already configured their Meebo account to remember the account information for their AIM, Yahoo!, etc. accounts. In this way, it works just like the other multi-protocol clients discussed earlier except that it is entirely web-based. It is worth mentioning that there are many single-protocol web-based clients as well. For instance, there are web-based versions of AIM and Yahoo! Messenger.

**Figure 4.4** Meebo web-based client

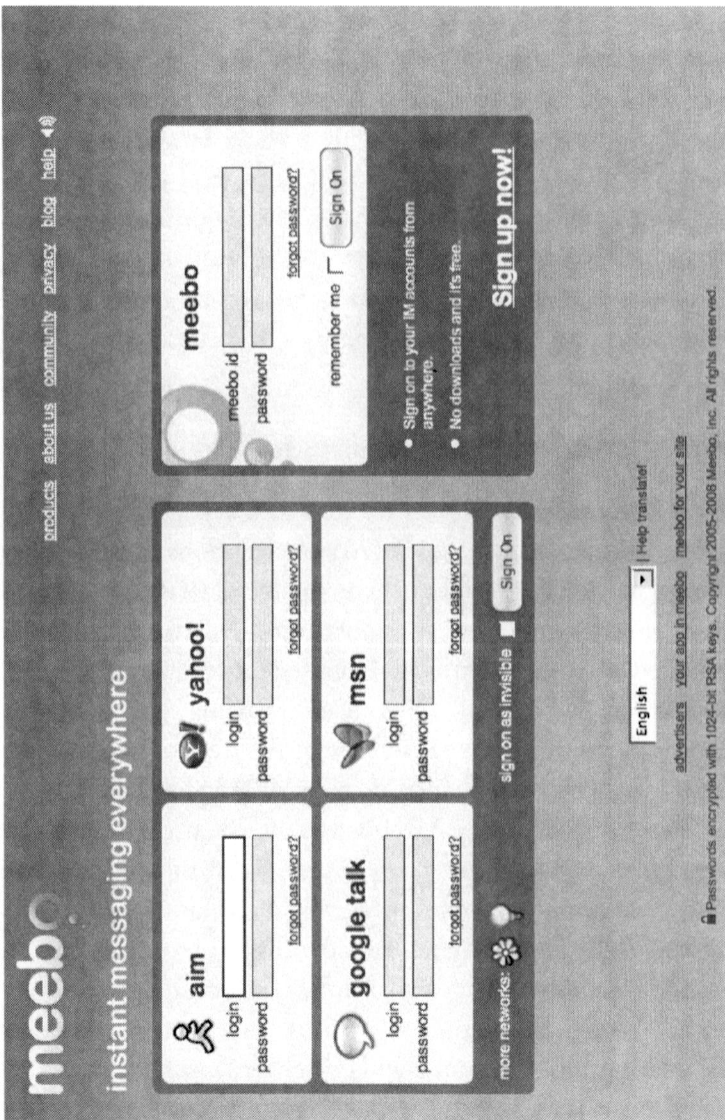

The Meebo client has several advantages:

- very easy to use;
- no need to install or customize software;
- it is not tied to a computer – users can log in from wherever they are.

But Meebo also has some 'cons':

- users must keep the browser window open;
- not as feature rich as most IM clients;
- 'new message' alerts can be fairly subtle – easy to miss;
- can be more difficult to manage multiple conversations as the chat windows are all inside the web browser window;
- Meebo will be going to an ad-supported model soon.

## Features

This might be a hard one to answer when you're first starting your IM reference service. Our advice is don't fret too much about the feature set of your IM client when you're getting started. As you work with it you'll get a sense of your own unique local needs. It isn't a big deal to change IM clients down the line, once everyone is comfortable with the basic practice of IM reference.

There are a wide variety of features out there.

- *File transferring.* Most IM clients provide some way for you to transfer files over the IM network. This is useful if you want to share a document with someone while you're chatting. However, we'd recommend that you set a policy against accepting files from patrons (discussed further in the policies section).

- *Graphic emoticons.* Love them or hate them, emoticons – those smiles and frowns created by characters on the keyboard – are a part of IM culture. They certainly aren't very professional, but they do help to convey feelings in an environment devoid of body language. Most IM clients provide optional 'graphical emoticons': when you type a colon and close parenthesis to indicate smiling, the program will automatically turn it into a yellow smiley-face.
- *Plug-ins/add-ins.* Some clients provide the ability for third-party and/or proprietary plug-ins to enhance the feature set further. For example, you can get plug-ins for Pidgin to do anything from changing the way you get notifications to sending you a text message when you get an IM and you're away from your computer! Once you're up and running, see what plug-ins are available. Remember, there will, almost by definition, be more plug-ins available for open source clients than for proprietary clients.
- *Voice messaging.*
- *Message logging.* If you think you might like to log your IM reference chats, you'll want to explore how the IM client handles message logging. Are the logs easy to find? To read? To delete? How are they organized?
- *Webcam support.*
- *Offline messaging.* Offline messaging – the ability to send a message to a contact who is not currently signed in, to be delivered when they do log in – is actually something that is supported (or not) at the protocol level. However, the client determines how this feature works, and sometimes has functionality that emulates offline messaging even for protocols that do not support it. You probably won't have much call to use this, but it's worth checking out.
- *Spellcheck.*

## Open source versus proprietary

Many libraries like to support open source software whenever possible. Is it important to your library to use an open source product? Conversely, are you more comfortable with proprietary software? Keep in mind that proprietary software is often better documented and is designed with an average customer in mind. Open source software can be less well supported and/or less straightforward to work with. That said, the major open source IM client at the time of writing, Pidgin, is quite mature and is widely used in libraries. We feel confident that you'll have no problems getting the support you need in using it.

## Operating system

Your choice of client will be narrowed by the platform you use. Adium is lovely software but it won't do you any good if you don't have a Mac. Likewise, Digsby is getting great reviews, but isn't yet available for Mac or Linux.

## Cost/advertisements

Most IM clients are free but some, like Trillian Pro, make more features available if you purchase the professional or premium version. Other clients might be free but supported by advertising.

## Encryption

We discuss encryption options for increased privacy in Chapter 9. If making encryption an option is a priority for you, you'll want to choose a client that supports it.

## Setting up the software

Instant messaging software really requires very little in the way of set-up. Once you have created your accounts and selected a client, you're ready to get going.

### *Enter your accounts*

Enter your account information into the client. This should be a fairly straightforward process, but does vary from client to client. Figure 4.5 shows a screenshot from the account set-up process in Adium.

**Figure 4.5** **Adding an account to Adium**

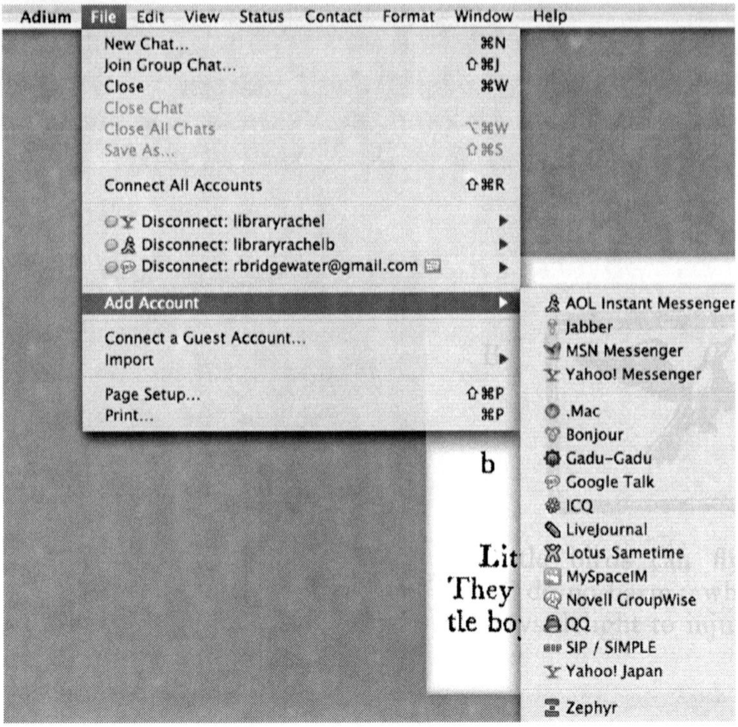

**Figure 4.6** Adding an account

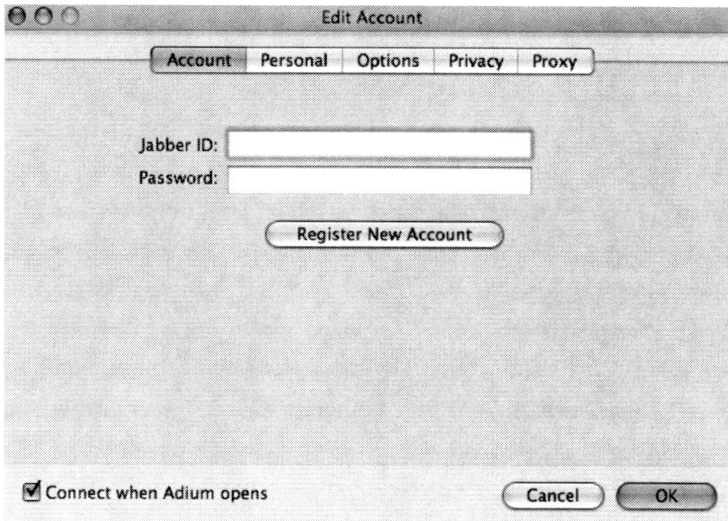


The user chooses 'Add Account' and then selects the kind of account she would like to add (e.g. AOL, Yahoo!, Jabber). She will then be prompted to add her user name/ID and password for that account (Figure 4.6).

That's it! The account is set up! Note in Figure 4.6 that 'Connect when Adium opens' is selected. Look for a setting like this when you are setting up your accounts to ensure that the accounts connect automatically when you start the software. A customization you might want to look for from the start is the 'avatar' (or 'icon'). The 'avatar' is the little picture that appears near your name when you are chatting on IM. If your library has a logo, you might want to use that.

## Preferences

You will quickly discover that there are a great number of preferences you can set with most clients. Most of them don't matter all that much and you can play around with your configurations to your heart's content. There are, however, some configuration settings you'll want to pay attention to from the start.

## Notifications, especially sounds

Most IM clients alert you to a new message using some combination of window behavior and sounds. In most library settings, audible alerts simply will not do. That said, most computers in these settings likely have the volume muted in any case. Silencing audible alerts is probably a good idea. Next, see what the options are for notifications and play around with each of them. Do you like it when the window pops in front of what you're working on? Do you want a separate notification window to pop up somewhere on the screen? Is a simple, flashing task bar icon sufficient to get your attention? See what's available in the client you've selected, and don't forget to ask your staff for their preferences too!

## Multiple windows versus tabs in a single window

Many clients will give you the option of having a new window for each active chat or, instead, conducting new chats in tabs within one window, as shown in Figure 4.7. This is purely a matter of preference. Some people can't stand having multiple windows open, others like keeping each conversation in its own window.

## Message logging

The pros and cons of logging your chats are discussed at length elsewhere in this book. Just remember to adjust this setting to reflect the policy you've set regarding message logging.

**Figure 4.7** **New conversation open in tabs**

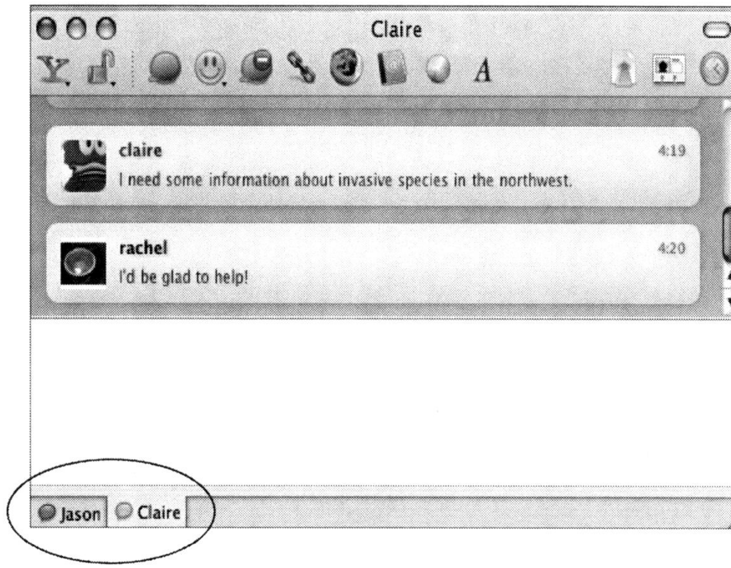


## Status messages

Status messages are a way for you to augment the basic available/away/offline presence indicators with additional information about your availability. Remember that it is possible to set up any number of custom status messages. Depending on your situation (how you're staffing the service, etc.), we recommend that you set up some of the following to get started.

- An 'available' message that says something like 'Ask us a question!' This will help your patrons feel welcomed. Use this as your standard 'available' status.
- An 'away' message that says something like 'We're busy helping other patrons right now.' You could add additional notes to that message, as well, instructing people to check back later or to go ahead and ask a question but know that

there might be a delay in your response. If things get busy at the desk you can quickly change your status to this message. This allows you to give the best possible service to the people in front of you and to ensure that IM patrons are not left hanging on.

- An 'away' message that says 'We've stepped away from the desk for a moment.' You could also make a habit of editing that status message whenever you use it to reflect when you plan to be back to the desk.

Be creative! Remember, you can also change your status messages to reflect special goings-on in the library. Having an open house? Create an 'available' message that says something like 'Free cookies in the library today.'

## Getting your first IM

We hope you will have experimented using IM for communicating with co-workers, colleagues, friends and family before you take your first IM question. However, we couldn't write a book about IM reference without talking a bit about the flow of conversation in an IM dialog.

When a patron is requesting a chat session with you, a chat window will pop up, flash or otherwise get your attention (Figure 4.8). The specific way that the chat window will get your attention will depend upon the software you've selected (the client) and the preferences you've set. Typically, a window will pop up in front of whatever you're working on. It is also possible, if the person has added you to their contact list, that you will get an authorization request confirming that it is okay to be added to their list (Figure 4.9). You'll definitely want to authorize this! After all, being on their contact list is what you

**Figure 4.8** Getting a message

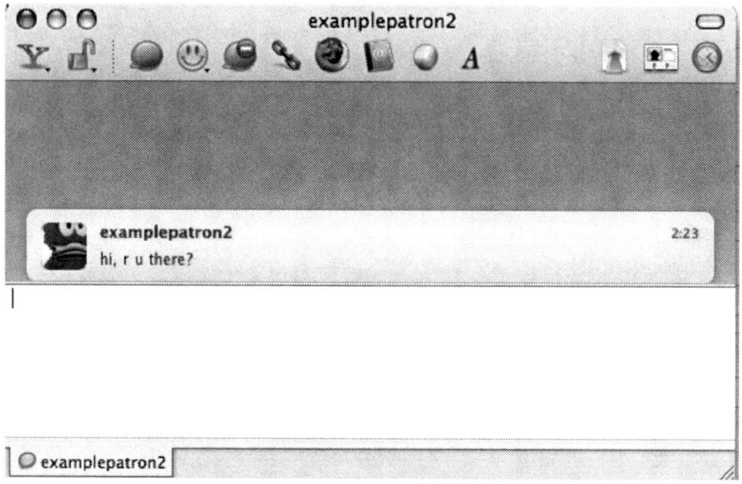


**Figure 4.9** An authorization request

want! As a matter of policy, you should probably *not* add the patron to the library's contact list. You won't be initiating conversations with your patrons, and it offers greater protection of their privacy if you leave them off your list.

By typing in the lower window of the chatbox, you'll be able to respond to the patron (Figure 4.10). The patron

**Figure 4.10** Responding to a chat

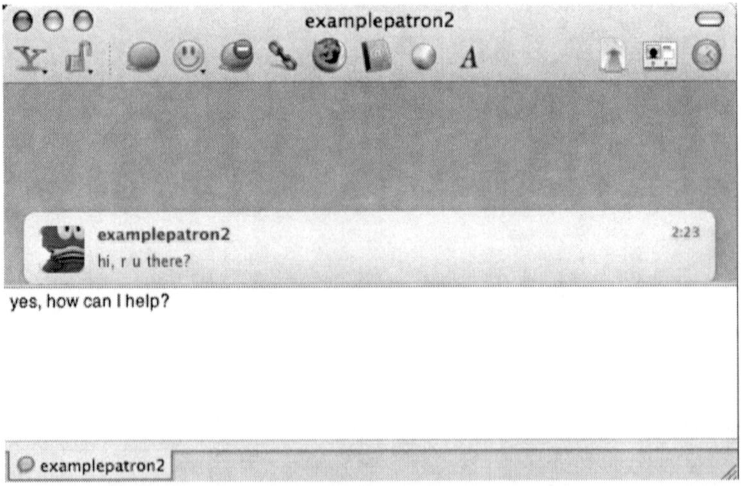


**Figure 4.11** The chat window indicates when you are typing

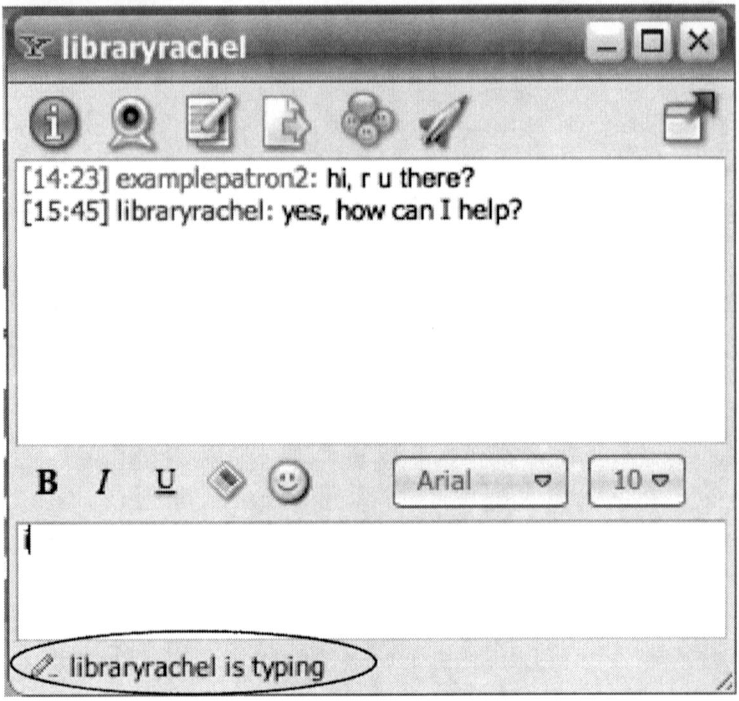

cannot see what you've written until you send it. You send the message either by just hitting 'return' on your keyboard or, with some software, hitting a 'send' button on the window. Depending on how you have things configured, the patron will see that you are typing while you're typing but he will not see what you are typing. Figure 4.11 shows a Meebo window with the typing indicated on the bottom status bar. This will look slightly different in all clients.

After you have sent your message, it will appear in the top window (Figure 4.12).

Then you repeat the process. That's really all there is to it! When the conversation is over you can simply close the window.

**Figure 4.12** Chat in progress

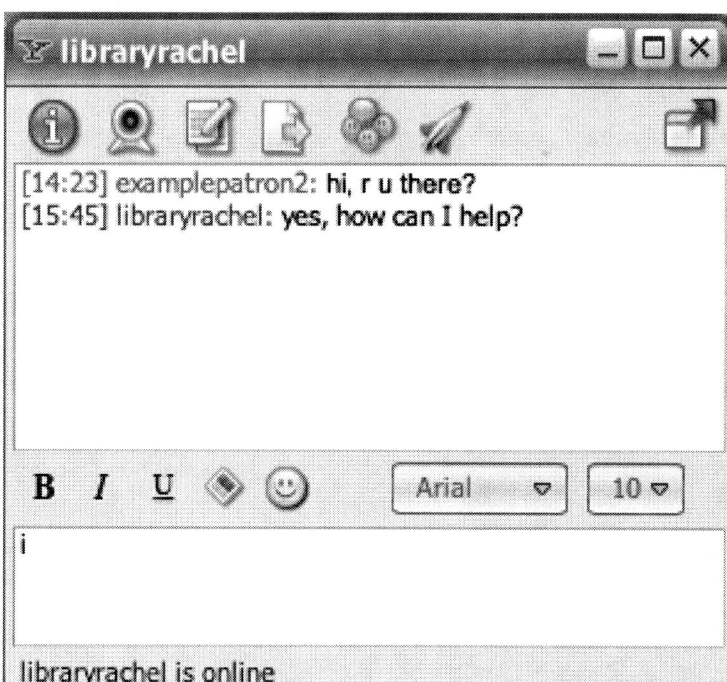

# Staffing

One of the first things you need to figure out when you decide to start an IM reference service is how you will staff it, at least initially. You need to make this decision up front because it will drive other decisions you make down the line.

- Take IMs on the reference desk.
- Librarians rotate taking IMs in their offices/cubicles.
- Take IMs in a third location.

## *Take IMs on the reference desk*

Many libraries will be able to add IM references to the duties of the person/people staffing their reference desks. This is an especially reasonable option for libraries with fairly slow public desks.

- *Pro.* Very straightforward scheduling. Librarian has easy access to reference collection. Make better use of staff time currently being underutilized. Only one (or few) software installation to maintain. Can easily monitor logs (if desired). IM hours tied to in-person reference hours.
- *Con.* Librarian will need to balance in-person patrons with IM patrons. Can be overwhelming if it gets busy. Potentially less private. IM hours tied to in-person reference hours. All librarians who staff the desk must participate or procedures must be developed to accommodate those who don't.

## *Librarians rotate taking IMs in their offices/cubicles*

- *Pro.* Librarian will not need to balance IMs with live patrons. Participation can be limited to only certain librarians. IM reference hours can easily be different from in-person hours. Librarians can opt for the IM client that they like best (if the use of a web-based client is not mandated).
- *Con.* Additional schedule must be created. 'Hand-offs' throughout the day can be complicated. Librarian does not have easy access to reference collection. Though the librarian can work on other things, she will have to deal with interruptions – possibly less productive during IM shifts. Software must be maintained in multiple locations or a web-based client must be used. Away messages, generic responses, etc., must be maintained in multiple locations (or a web-based client must be used).

## *Take IMs in a third location*

Depending on the size, reference traffic and menu of services offered by your library, you may already have a location away from the public reference desk where 'virtual', telephone and e-mail reference services are offered. In this case it would likely make sense simply to add IM to the responsibilities of the person staffing this location.

Libraries not already possessing a desk/area for these kinds of services might feel that adding IM reference service warrants the creation of one. This option provides you with most of the positive aspects of the 'reference desk' option without the stress of balancing IM with face-to-face patrons. However, if such a desk doesn't already exist, you will be creating an additional service point that will need to be staffed.

When Jenna Ryan, a librarian at Louisiana State University, posted this clear description of the IM reference set-up at her library to the DIG-REF list-serv, we immediately got in touch with her to see if she would be willing to share it with our readers. We hope reading about Jenna's IM set-up will give you ideas for your own.

> We use Meebo widgets embedded on our Virtual Reference page, www.lib.lsu.edu/virtual/onlinereference.html, as well as on the 'no results' page in our catalog search and a few other places where we feel people might need immediate help. The widgets, along with AIM, Yahoo! and MSN screen names, are collectively monitored using Pidgin, www.pidgin.im/ (which some of you might recognize as having once been called Gaim). We used Pam Sessoms's wonderful tutorial for setting Pidgin up to monitor the widgets and for working around the pesky authorization requests: www.lib.unc.edu/reference/eref/pidgin/meebomewidget.html.
>
> The Pidgin program files are actually stored on our local server, and installed on each librarian's computer from that location, so that when the logs are stored, they are all stored in that central folder, rather than on the individual desktops of the people monitoring the service.
>
> Simply clicking on 'Tools' then 'Preferences' then 'Logging' in the Pidgin window shows three check boxes. We have the first two (instant messaging and chat) checked, with the third (system messages) unchecked. That way our logs aren't filled up with lots of 'so and so is idle' messages and such. The logs are automatically stored in a subfolder with the program files. Once a week or so, we have a graduate assistant go

through the logs and enter information like date, time begun, time ended and chat status (completed, unanswered, after hours, etc.) into an Excel spreadsheet (which I'd be happy to send to anyone who wants a copy, but can and should be altered to fit your own statistical needs). I am able to go back in later and manipulate the data however necessary using Excel functions. Since we generally get about ten chats a week, it's really not that onerous a chore for the grad student.

We also use several standard plug-ins in Pidgin to make our lives easier. Plug-ins are found under 'Tools' then 'Plugins' on the Pidgin menu. With the exception of the auto-authorization plug-in, which can be downloaded from Pam Sessoms's page referenced above, all of the following come standard with the Pidgin program.

*Timestamp*: checking this box automatically provides an hour:minute:second timestamp for each line of chat, which shows up both during the chat session and in the stored log. This lets the operator know exactly when the last statement was sent, as well as allowing anyone viewing the log to tell how long a chat session took.

*Text replacement*: checking this box enables the text replacement feature. Highlighting the plug-in and clicking on the 'configure plugin' button allows you to alter the settings. The standard settings are things like replacing 'teh' with 'the' and 'adn' with 'and'. The plug-in allows you to set custom replacements though, and this is where the real usefulness is. For example, we have the plug-in set to replace '/1' with 'Hello. Welcome to LSU Libraries. How may we help you?' Any number of pre-scripted statements and responses can be programmed, including URLs that will automatically become links when posted. Just remember to make whatever designation you give to the macro something you won't find yourself typing in a normal situation.

There are several other options in the plug-ins – for example 'Notification settings' allows you to determine whether you want the chat window to come to the fore automatically when someone IMs you or if you just want the window on the task bar to flash.

For the past year we have had a staff of about ten librarians and grad assistants staffing the VR from their desks in one-hour shifts, Monday through Thursday from 9 to 5. However, scheduling is getting increasingly difficult as we have lost some of our staff members and people are getting busier. As such, we have decided to move staffing to the reference desk at least on a trial basis. We usually have two people working the reference desk at a time, and neither VR nor regular desk traffic is usually so busy that both could not be handled simultaneously. In addition, this allows us to have longer VR hours, since someone will be at the reference desk for most of the day.

Right now the statistics that I process are on a monthly basis, including most popular days/times, average chat length and number of completed chats versus those that are attempted during off hours or accidentally unanswered or abandoned by either librarian or student. Luckily the latter are very low, at least on our part, and only once in the past year have we had a session disconnected or unanswered due to technical difficulties with either Meebo or Pidgin. Compared to the nearly 50 per cent disconnect rate we had with the proprietary software we were using before we switched, I have been 'very' happy with the results. (Jenna Ryan, Middleton Library, Louisiana State University)

# Training

We can practically guarantee you that the training necessary to prepare your staff to provide IM service will be minimal, especially in this very basic set-up that we describe. The amount of training needed will vary depending on the comfort level of your staff. If you have staff members who IM every day with their friends, they might not need any training at all in using the software and will merely need to be brought up to speed on local policies and practices!

## Some tips for training staff for IM reference

- *Have staff chat with one another prior to making your service available to patrons.* As with so many things, IM is best learned by doing! Encourage staffers to install IM on their work machines or to use a web-based IM client and chat with one another. This kind of practice is the best training for IM.
- *Create a list of common 'IM-speak' or use the one included in this book.* Many librarians are nervous about IM because they've heard that users employ a confusing shorthand in their communications. While it is true that the typical IM patron will probably use such shorthand as 'R' for 'are' and 'U' for 'you', this 'IM-speak' is rarely all that confusing. That said, providing librarians with the tools they will need to decipher any cryptic codes can be a great stress reliever.
- *Stage IM sessions in staff meetings and one-on-one.* Show a typical IM session in a staff meeting (note: you'll need a willing accomplice on the other end). Do this again in one-on-one sessions with librarians who will be providing the service. Answer any questions they have about the software.

- *Be clear about any policies, including chat logging*. If you plan to log chats for statistical, training or other reasons, be sure to tell your staff. It can be very intimidating to have a record created of a reference transaction; you need to let them know if you're doing it and why. If you have any policies – formal or informal – regarding the use of IM for reference services, be sure that all staff are made aware of them.

Minimally, all staff need to be able to:

- start the software up/sign in;
- respond to a chat request;
- change status;
- sign off.

## Policies

What kinds of policies do you need surrounding IM reference services? Naturally, these will vary from library to library, and the policies you need to have in place for your IM service will be determined, in large part, by the demands of your environment. That said, there are a number of policy areas you can consider as you get started:

- harassment;
- service population;
- security;
- staff use of IM;
- records retention;
- public computing.

## Harassment

You absolutely should have a policy regarding harassment over IM. Fortunately, you probably already have formal or informal policies regarding appropriate patron behavior in the library and can simply transfer those policies to your IM service. We strongly believe that any behavior that would not be acceptable in person is not acceptable on IM.

## Service population

When you start offering IM reference services, especially if you use a widget on your website, you will likely be surprised by how many seemingly random people IM you with questions. It is likely that you will get questions, at least occasionally, from people who are not part of your service population. You'll need to decide what level of IM reference service is appropriate to offer these patrons.

## Security

The biggest security risk with IM is the threat of viruses and worms. There are some common-sense policies you can put into place to help prevent exposure to security threats. The best thing you can do is to set a policy against accepting file transfers from patrons. There's not much reason why they should need to send files to you, and you really have no way of knowing what is in the file before they send it.

## Staff use of IM

Depending on your environment, it might make sense to set some policies or guidelines about how staff should use IM in the workplace. Some employers resist implementing IM because of the specter of employees tucked away in their offices furtively chatting with their friends and families all day. It is certainly true that having an IM identity makes you available to the rest of the world in a way that you otherwise would not be. If this is a concern, it might be sensible to align your IM policy with your e-mail policy. Recognize that IM conversations are much like face-to-face conversations and an IM with a colleague about important work concerns is likely also to include a certain amount of chit-chat and personal conversation, just as there would be if they met over coffee.

## Records retention

Records retention policies are required when dealing with chat logs. If you should decide to log your chats, you should have policies governing:

- how long the logs will be kept;
- what they will be used for;
- who will have access to them.

Please note that many instant messages at some institutions (especially government bodies and corporations) may be governed by institutional records retention policies, like e-mail and other communications.

## Public computing

Finally, some libraries have rules about how their public computers can be used that forbid the use of chat. Libraries instituting chat reference will probably want to reconsider such policies.

## Building FSU Libraries' IM reference service

Below is the text of a chat Meryl had with Dawn Lowe-Wincentsen of Florida State University Libraries about the evolution of her library's IM reference service.

> Dawn: We moved to IM last May (2006). We had done a study on the number of questions we were getting and who they were from as part of the consortial service we were participating in, and found we were not really getting any of our own patrons... so we wanted a service that would be easy to use, and be for FSU. We figured IM was something most undergraduates – our target population – were familiar with anyway, so we went with it.
>
> Meryl: Was the consortial service IM or chat?
>
> Dawn: Our original service was started in spring of 2003 using the QuestionPoint service... chat... and the service at the time was average... we just wanted something that was better for our users... It was also cheaper and easier for the staff to use... When we switched to IM we started off using Trillian which we put on a shared drive and people logged on and could use it from their offices... It is another multi-service platform, but we chose it because it would allow us to keep the logs and use those for statistical and training purposes.
>
> Meryl: How many librarians staff your service at any one time? Is that why it's convenient for them to access it from their offices?
>
> Dawn: With Meebo anyone providing service can access it from anywhere... it is one of the benefits as we

have a few people who do VR on evenings or weekends from home – myself included.

Meryl: Ohhhh.

Dawn: We have one person at a time online though we have an IM network in-house (we use AIM) and they can refer questions that way if they need to... The Meebo widget was something we started looking into in February of this year... One of the technology people and myself started talking about it, and finding a work around for taking the statistics... He – Mason, the tech guy – developed a stat bot.

Meryl: I follow.

Dawn: This is a bot that asks how many questions you have had each hour the service is active and sends me an e-mail at the end of the day... it also sends me a note if someone is not logged on... or if someone didn't answer it... This could be used with anything as it is just an AIM ID programmed to ask how many questions... so we tested it with Trillian, then we moved to Meebo, then implanted the widgets in the website.

Meryl: OK.

Dawn: The people staffing the service like Meebo better than QuestionPoint or Trillian... it is easier to get into, and our service has drastically picked up since implanting the widget.

Meryl: Really? Do you think it's because of the visibility?

Dawn: Note: I say people instead of librarians as we use trained staff more than traditional MLIS holders to staff our service... The pick-up in stats is definitely visibility... we get many people that see it on the site and just click on it to check if it works or not.

Meryl: Do you use that time to explain/market the service?

Dawn: Yes, or just to be friendly and try to alleviate any anxieties they may have... we also market the service through our instruction classes.

Meryl: Got it.

Dawn: And have ads in a planner that every student gets free.

Meryl: Nice touch.

Dawn: Our staff volunteer for the service, as do our librarians. This alleviates any issue with people who are uncomfortable with technology or otherwise not willing to provide the service.

Meryl: Did/do you provide any training?

Dawn: We do a show and tell each time there is a change and allow those interested to provide feedback... this summer we have had weekly training by subject on resources for both the reference desk staff and the VR staff.

Meryl: By respective subject specialists?

Dawn: When available the training is by specialists.

Meryl: How would you rate the traffic on your service?

Dawn: Probably about average.

Meryl: Do you still receive e-mail ref questions?

Dawn: Last month – a summer month – we had 80-something questions.

Meryl: That's not bad at all for a summer month... Mostly undergrads? Or can you tell?

Dawn: We do still get e-mail... there is not a way to tell who is using the service, but the questions vary by difficulty from where is a book to how do I search for X... sometimes when a faculty member asks a question they will identify themselves as Dr Smith from History or such.

Meryl: Do you have 'canned' responses? Otherwise questioners (odd word) don't ID themselves?

Dawn: Besides the odd faculty member we do not get a lot of people identifying themselves... and if people have a circ question we discourage them from identifying themselves over IM or the phone and encourage them to come in.

Meryl: For security?

Dawn: Just for reasons of confidentiality.

Meryl: Sure.

Dawn: We still have SSNs [social security numbers] involved in some things and we do not want the numbers freely passed about.

Meryl: Oh. Of course... Overall, are you happy with your VR service? And where do you see it going?

Dawn: I think our service is just getting off the ground... I would like to expand it in the future, but I want to see how well it does in its current incarnation for the fall semester.

Meryl: Expand how?

Dawn: And technically speaking I am not sure how we would expand... but I would like to find a way to have more than one person online at once.

Meryl: I see.

Dawn: And to have later hours, possibly after the library closes even (2am is semester close time)... We get the majority of questions from 4pm to close.

Meryl: Chat soon...

## Summary

As you can see, getting started with IM reference is really just a matter of getting your accounts set up, downloading some easy-to-use software, taking a little while to get familiar with it and doing a little thinking about the policies you'll need. There's more you can do, and probably more you will do, but all of those more advanced things can be safely left until you have your feet wet. Remember, one reason that IM is so popular is that it's easy and fun!

5

# Conducting the IM reference interview

> The reference interview is essentially a conversation between a reference staff member and a user, the goal of which is to ascertain the user's information need and take appropriate action to satisfy that need through skillful use of available information sources… Care is required to avoid misunderstanding the user's need or prematurely assuming one has fully understood it. Similar care must be taken in developing the correct strategy for a successful search of the available information sources to meet that need. Then the librarian must evaluate the information found and communicate its nature and value to the user in a helpful and understandable manner. Finally, the librarian must ensure that, in the opinion of the user, the information provided fully answers the question. (Bopp, 2001: 47)

In Chapter 4 we looked at getting your IM client downloaded and set up, and went over the basics of how an IM reference session will work from a software perspective. Mastering the software, though, is a relatively minor part of offering IM reference. Just as important is being comfortable with the transactions themselves. How is providing IM reference different from face-to-face reference? What do you need to look out for? How can you be most successful? This chapter will guide you through the IM reference transaction. We want you to remember, though, that there's no special magic to this. At the end of the day, IM reference is, well, reference. Use the same skills, tricks, experiences, knowledge and compassion as you use in face-to-face reference and you can't help but do well! Table 5.1 gives some basic guidelines for working with IM.

Conducting an effective reference interview is a vital skill in any librarian's toolbox. We are taught how best to draw patrons out, since we are also taught that patrons might very well not be asking the question for which they truly want an answer. The literature advocates open-ended (neutral) questioning and closed questioning to get at the 'real' question, but advises using one or the other only at specified times during the reference interview. Remember, at all times, that talking to a user online is substantially similar to talking

**Table 5.1** **IM guidelines**

| |
|---|
| ▪ Break responses up into one- or two-line segments |
| ▪ Interrupting is part of IM, don't worry about it |
| ▪ Questions and answers fall on top of each other – that is both fine and expected |
| ▪ Common abbreviations are accepted |
| ▪ Typos are expected so don't waste too much time correcting yours, just make sure your intent is clear |
| ▪ Many younger users will use abbreviations; try not to use them so that you maintain a level playing field with all users |
| ▪ Often, but not always, IMers are multitasking so lag time is okay and expected, but be sure to maintain contact |
| ▪ As with e-mail, ALL CAPS is considered yelling |
| ▪ Follow the patron's lead |
| ▪ Indicate emphasis by *asterisks* or underlining |

to one face to face, but that you may need to make a few adjustments to your approach to accommodate the medium of communication. For example, in face-to-face reference you are able to rely on body language to help you translate the answer to a neutral question. The 'virtual' interview might require more direct and/or closed questioning than a face-to-face interview, because tone of voice and body language are taken out of the equation. Don't allow your commitment to a certain style of reference interview prevent your IM conversation from being just that, a conversation.

Much of the literature likens the reference interview to a diagnostic conversation with a doctor – since the patron/patient is describing symptoms and the librarian/doctor is asking questions to clarify the information need/condition. The analogy serves well, for it reminds us that reference interviews are, again, just conversations to determine what information is sought. In the book *Reference and Information Services*, Bopp (2001: 48) distills the reference interview down to three basic and straightforward steps.

- Gain the trust of the user.
- Ascertain from the user an accurate understanding of the question, so that it can be answered as completely as possible.
- Make sure that the user is satisfied with the answer provided.

Why all the emphasis on basic, straightforward and distilled? Because in a virtual reference interview, simplicity can be the key to success! Let's digress briefly to assess how we define a successful reference interview: one in which the patron is satisfied with the service. Ideally, the user will also be satisfied with the resulting information and with the librarian. Either way, the most important and salient measure of good service is a satisfied customer who will, hopefully, return. Let's not assume that there is a direct correlation between the amount of time we spend with a patron and their satisfaction with the encounter – in reference, either face to face or virtual, quantity does not equal quality.

To frame our discussion of the virtual reference interview, we use the five steps Bopp (ibid.) outlines for face-to-face reference interviews, since the principles are the same.

- Opening the interview.
- Negotiating the question.
- The search process.
- Communicating information to the user.
- Closing the interview.

Further, we referred to RUSA's *Guidelines for Behavioral Performance of Reference and Information Service Providers* (American Library Association, 2004) and the Virtual Reference Desk (2003) 'Facets of quality' to enhance our discussion and highlight the virtual component. Finally, throughout this section we refer to Figure 5.1, a sample IM reference interview between MarcusBrown and IMRefDesk at an academic library. References are indicated by the tag 'Observe: IMRefDesk indicator X'.

## Opening the interview: setting the stage with your website

If you are seeking information and the person you approach is friendly and welcoming, you feel more comfortable. If you are lost and approach a gas-station attendant who smiles as

**Figure 5.1** **Sample chat with Marcus Brown**

**MarcusBrown**: hello?
(A) **IMRefDesk**: Hi! I'm Jamie, the reference librarian. How can I help you?
**MarcusBrown**: i need some stuff about logging
(B) **IMRefDesk**: That's an interesting topic. Is there a particular aspect of logging that you're looking at?
**MarcusBrown**: i need some information about the harmful effects
**MarcusBrown**: my teacher says i can't use websites
**IMRefDesk**: Oh, OK, what kind of class is this for?
(C) **MarcusBrown**: it's for my environmental studies class
**IMRefDesk**: Have you found any resources yet?
**MarcusBrown**: no i don't really where to start looking
**IMRefDesk**: OK, well, let's get you started looking for some journal articles.
**IMRefDesk**: To find articles you'll need to use the article databases.
**IMRefDesk**: Are you a student at the university? You'll need to be in order to access our databases from off campus.
**MarcusBrown**: yes
**IMRefDesk**: Great. And are you familiar with the library's databases?
**MarcusBrown**: yep.
**IMRefDesk**: OK. Click on 'databases' from the library homepage.
**MarcusBrown**: What one do i use?
**IMRefDesk**: We have a few that might be useful. You could start out with Environment Complete.
**IMRefDesk**: Why don't you start poking around in there and while you're doing that I will try some things and get back to you.
**IMRefDesk**: Let me know if you have any questions about using Environment Complete. I'll be back with you in a couple of minutes.
**MarcusBrown**: kewl, thx!
(D) **MarcusBrown**: all this stuff is about the rainforest, i need stuff about around here.
**MarcusBrown**: i mean, stuff about the US
**IMRefDesk**: One thing I noticed after I'd seen some of my results from my first couple searches was that a lot of the articles used the subject heading 'LOGGING – Environmental Aspects'.
(E) **IMRefDesk**: You can try that search by putting 'LOGGING – Environmental Aspects' in the search box and choosing SU – Subject Terms from the 'Select a Field' pulldown.
**MarcusBrown**: oh i see what you mean.
**MarcusBrown**: how do i make it just the us?

**Figure 5.1** **Sample chat with Marcus Brown (*Cont'd*)**

**IMRefDesk**: If you look on the left side of the screen you'll see you can narrow it by adding on some terms, one of the choices is 'United States', try that.
**MarcusBrown**: oh okay, cool.
(F) **IMRefDesk**: Great! At a glance do the article titles look like the information will be helpful and will allow you to see the issue from both perspectives?
**MarcusBrown**: yep.
**IMRefDesk**: Super. Keep poking around in the databases and if you get stuck, please don't hesitate to contact us again.
(G) **IMRefDesk**: Also, you mentioned that you wanted books. I can help you search for books in our catalog whenever you're ready. You might also want to just come in and browse around our Environmental Information Cooperative collection.
**MarcusBrown**: thanks! i have to go to class... this is good tho.
**IMRefDesk**: OK. Have a good class! Thanks for chatting with us!
**MarcusBrown**: k bye

you get closer, you feel less upset that you are lost. If you approach the reference desk for information and the librarian smiles as you get closer, again you feel better and more assured about your question. Just as in any service encounter, librarians (service providers) must create comfortable ground so that patrons feel free to ask their questions. We've all read up on how to make reference desks more inviting – by design, placement, signage, smiles and so on. How do we translate these welcome signs to the virtual environment?

## *Make it visible!*

RUSA's *Guidelines* suggest 'placing contact information for chat, email, telephone, and other services in prominent locations'. Currently there are two ways libraries are handling this: a link on the homepage to a contact us/ask us page and a widget directly on the front page. First let's talk about the link method. Most libraries offering virtual reference have an obvious link on their homepage that leads to a contact us/ask us page. It is important that this link is extraordinarily apparent so that patrons can locate it easily and they know the service is available.

Some libraries use a widget on their front page so that patrons can immediately IM the reference librarian without signing in or downloading software. Widgets are immediate and therefore appealing to many IMers. Be aware, however, of the limitations: some widgets require the patron to remain on the page while chatting. The patron cannot, in other words, browse while waiting to hear back from the librarian. Oregon State University Libraries (http://osulibrary.oregonstate.edu/) is one of many libraries that have solved this problem by replacing the 'live' widget with an image of the widget (Figure 5.2). When the user clicks on the image of the chat widget, a new window opens for the chat. Some widgets are just beginning to roll out technology that will allow the widget box to 'follow' the user from page to page on the website, but this is not yet commonplace.

Regardless of the method used, the contact us/ask us page should contain the same useful information:

- clear and brief instructions;
- all reference desk screen names;
- alternative methods for contacting the reference desk (in person, e-mail, phone, fax);
- hours the IM service is staffed;
- who the service serves.

## *Make it clear who you serve!*

In face-to-face interactions we have a general idea about whom we are serving. Perhaps not perfect, but close enough

**Figure 5.2** Oregon State University Libraries' website – the chat window is actually just an image of a widget

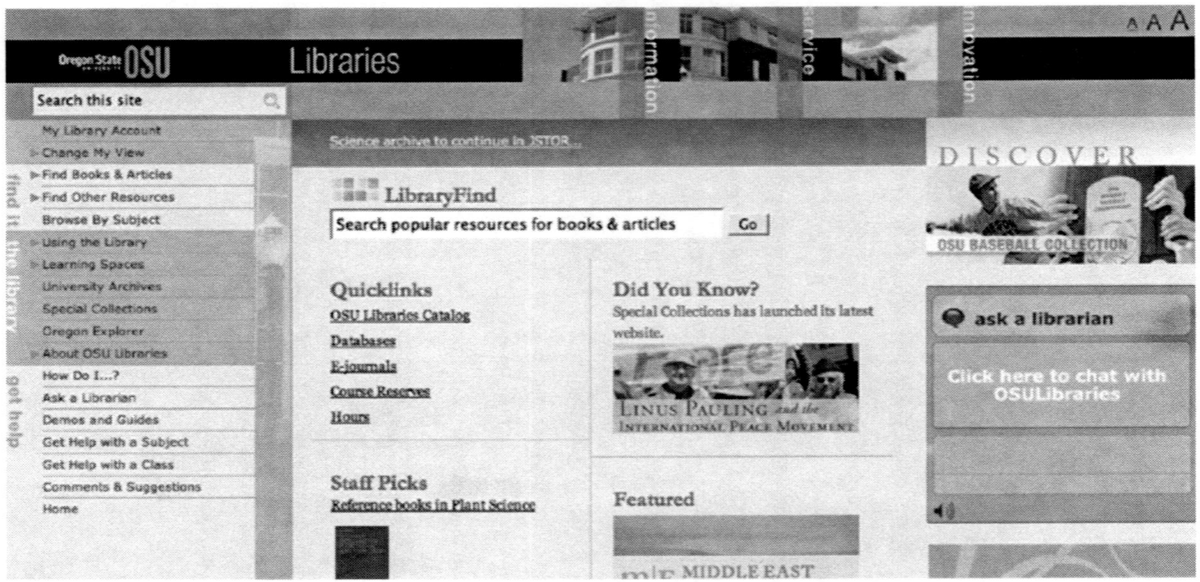

to help us help the patron and determine if the patron is part of our service population. In virtual interactions we simply cannot know who we are serving without asking questions that would compromise the patron's privacy. If you decide to set strict policies about whom you will serve using IM, it is best to notify people on your site. Yale Library's (www.library.yale.edu/reference/asklive/index.html) statement is exemplary (see Figure 5.3), as it indicates those it does (versus does not) serve, and even goes a step further, providing links to local libraries where you can get service if you are not part of the Yale community: 'Service is limited to Yale faculty, students,

**Figure 5.3** Yale University Library's service population statement

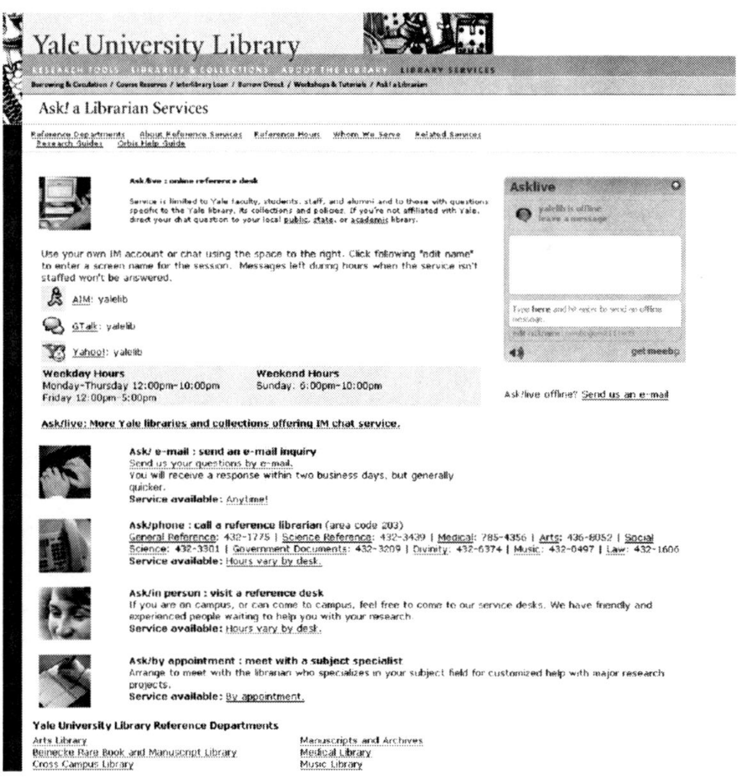

staff, and alumni and to those with questions specific to the Yale library, its collections and policies. If you're not affiliated with Yale, direct your chat question to your local public, state, or academic library.'

## *Make it usable and accessible!*

In talking about website design for IM reference, it is essential to talk briefly but explicitly about usability and accessibility issues. By now most of us are used to thinking of our websites as extensions of our service, even to the extent of considering them to be 'virtual branches'. If the website is a virtual branch, your IM reference service may very well be the 'reference desk' in that branch. So far we've addressed the need to be clear about our policies and the need to make the service easy to locate on our website. We can think of these things as equivalent to signage in our physical spaces. The usability and accessibility of our websites (specifically, the sections of those websites that pertain to our IM services) can be equated to the appearance and functionality of our physical reference desks. Just like we should think about how best to design our desks to make our patrons feel comfortable, we want to consider the design of our sites.

Usability refers to how smoothly a user can navigate a website, locate the function/information needed, use that function/information and remember how to do it next time. Most IMers generally spend only a few seconds looking for a site or information, so having an obvious, accessible and usable IM box is essential. Use consistent language to describe the service throughout your site (e.g. don't call it 'chat with a librarian' on one page and 'IM reference' on the next). Consistency will help your users locate and use the service. As always, avoid jargon whenever possible. Use status indicators (more on this in Chapter 4) to give your patrons instant information about your availability. Also, remember that most of your IM patrons will be visiting this part of your site only once or twice to get the information they need to add you to their buddy lists. With this in mind, make sure that your screen names are the most prominent information on the screen. There are many resources about website usability and about designing usability tests to determine if your site is up to snuff.

The accessibility of a site is related to how easy to use it is for disabled users. Users with limited vision might be using your website with a screen reader or with the text enlarged. Will your site be readable by such software? Can a person with limited mobility navigate your website using only the keyboard? Your website might already be regulated by government accessibility standards or you may already design for accessibility, but we felt it was worth mentioning here that just as we build our physical spaces to be usable and accessible to all of our patrons, we should take care when designing our virtual spaces.

### *Welcome the patron!*

Your links and widgets are in place, your contact page is complete, now welcome the patron! In the virtual reference environment, a brief hello, with the patron's name if possible and appropriate, goes a long way towards setting the stage for a successful reference interview. *Observe: IMRefDesk indicator A.*

- *Potential pitfall*: patron feels alienated by impersonal and brief nature of IM.
- *Remedy*: include friendly fragments in your responses, address patron by name and/or introduce yourself.

## Negotiating the question

Just as in a face-to-face reference transaction, when responding to IM reference questions you must attempt to elicit from the patron information about both the content of the question (what does she want to know) and about the constraints within which the patron is operating, such as the type of material wanted (article, website, book), depth of information preferred (elementary school, general interest) and any deadlines that are in place. Some chat services have these questions as part of their web-based query forms. In IM, however, there is no initial form that aids in gathering this practical information. And while necessary to help us deliver the best resources, given the potentially clinical nature of IM it would not do to fire these questions at the patron right off the bat. We need to establish rapport and exhibit interest first. Then move on to ascertain the depth of information. Next deliver a resource to gauge if you are going in the right direction. Repeat as needed!

In order to provide quality service, we know that we must demonstrate interest so that patrons feel comfortable. We all know, too, that demonstrating interest in patrons' questions in a virtual environment is not straightforward. When a patron is in front of us we can make eye contact, smile, nod and otherwise signal our interest. We need to find ways to translate these welcoming behaviors into an online conversation. Bell and Levy (2004: 149) believe the affective component greatly impacts reference service and advocate that 'librarians acknowledge questions with some level of emotion or a descriptive adjective in the first line. Some examples include "Good question," "Interesting topic," or "I'm sorry you are having trouble accessing our databases."' You may notice speakers employ this practice in town-hall meetings, for it acknowledges the questioner and gives you a moment to begin thinking. It is also a good way to maintain word contact with patrons, as RUSA recommends. *Observe: IMRefDesk indicator B.*

Your own library environment and unique patron base will help guide you as you decide what level of depth is appropriate. Public libraries have the most variability here. You could be working with an elementary school student or a business person. Try to use clues to get a first impression – the patron's tone and diction, for example. Remember, try not to make assumptions about the demographics of the person you're serving based on the fact that they are an IM user. While IM is certainly more popular with younger people, there is plenty of diversity among IM users. If you remain unsure, simply ask, just as you would if the patron was standing in front of you. Again, use clues from the patron to determine a more accurate level. *Observe: IMRefDesk indicator C.*

Next, try delivering a resource or discussing with the patron your plans for seeking a resource to ensure you understand what the patron is looking for. Once the patron indicates that you are on the right track, you can dig deeper. *Observe: IMRefDesk indicator D.*

Over the balance of the virtual reference interview, proceed as you would in a face-to-face interview, clarifying the information need, the type of resources sought, the timeline, etc. Just as in a face-to-face interaction, you'll want to be mindful of a user's privacy (see Chapter 9 for a discussion of privacy issues in IM).

We would remind you, again, that though there is information it would be useful to have from the patron, we must refrain from taking too much time asking questions. Ronan (2003: 45) advises that librarians should 'Strive to be friendly yet economical with your words.' This is not to say that you should give patrons short shrift; the balance is a tricky, yet manageable, one to strike between taking too much or too little time. Take advantage of open-ended questions to understand tone, since these questions can take the place of non-verbal signals. Closed questions, which we might use more sparingly in face-to-face reference, work well in the IM environment since they help to keep the transaction on point.

- *Potential pitfall*: conducting a reference interview that is too long.
- *Remedy*: recognize that closed questions often function better in a virtual environment, and use them more than you would in a face-to-face interview.

Bell and Levy (2004: 147) give a valuable table that demonstrates how to turn visible signals (facial expressions, gaze, body orientation and gestures, proxemics, clothes and appearance, paralanguage) into virtual signals. For example, facial expression is one way we communicate with patrons. Face to face, we can indicate helpfulness with a smile. Bell and Levy suggest 'Great question' as a virtual equivalent to that smile.

## The search process

Bopp (2001: 57) believes the search process 'should be a joint enterprise'. Just as the librarian and patron work together to negotiate the question, here they negotiate as well, comparing notes as the process unfolds to determine the fitness of the resources. It is this exchange, this feedback, which increases the likelihood of success!

Most librarians would agree that an ideal outcome of a reference transaction would be that the patron would not only have the information sought but would have learned how to search for and evaluate information in future. The

Virtual Reference Desk (2003) indicates that this is, in fact, part and parcel of the service: 'Quality digital reference services offer more to users than straight, factual answers; they guide them in how to formulate questions, subject knowledge, and information literacy.' Ideally, yes; practically, perhaps not. While we certainly must strive to provide the best service possible, we must recognize that patrons using IM are, again, often operating on a different timeline than face-to-face patrons. Thus we need to balance the amount of information/instruction we give with the time spent. There is also an inherent difference between library reference practices and patron expectations in reference.

- *Potential pitfall*: frustrating the patron with too much instruction when the patron simply wants an answer.
- *Remedy*: as you conduct your search, explain, in one line or less, how you are proceeding. This enables you to impart to the patron your search strategy while maintaining contact.
- *Potential pitfall*: rushing to provide an answer, any answer, so that patrons do not abandon the IM session.
- *Remedy*: send one resource to the patron to gauge if you are on the right track.

## Communicating information to the user

Throughout the reference transaction we are continually communicating information to the patron, as the patron is to us. At this culminating stage of the reference transaction, we must be mindful of two overlapping issues: first, ensuring that the patron has access to or knows how to access the resulting resources; and second, copyright.

## *Access the information!*

As you identify resources that will fill your patron's need, you must be mindful of access issues. Depending on the policies you have in place, you probably will not know if the patron is affiliated with your library, and therefore permitted to access subscription databases and other licensed content your library has purchased. It would be wise to find out early in the interaction whether or not the patron will be able to access your subscription content. If the patron is unaffiliated with your library or otherwise unable to access licensed content, you'll want focus your search on freely available material (e.g. sites on the open web). If the resource the patron needs is freely available content, not subject to license restrictions, simply provide the patron with a link. If you find materials in your physical collection, you can supply instructions for locating the item on the shelves or having it delivered to another location. If the useful information is found in your proprietary research databases, though, you will need to be aware of license issues.

Essential, here, is that you ensure that your directions are brief and clear and that, most importantly, the patron understands how to execute them. The patron's experience accessing library resources is an important factor. *Observe: IMRefDesk indicator E.*

- *Potential pitfall*: assuming a patron's experience with the library collection.
- *Remedy*: a simple 'Have you used our databases before?' is brief and will help determine your course of action.

## Closing the interview

There is little distinction to be made between closing out the face-to-face versus the virtual reference interview. RUSA (American Library Association, 2004) calls this stage 'follow-up', and its list of steps to take includes those we are familiar with, such as ensuring that the patron:

- has no further information need;
- has the necessary information to locate/access the resources identified;
- knows how to follow up or inquire further;
- knows that the reference desk is available.

Satisfactory follow-up can be a bit trickier in IM because the norms for concluding a conversation are much less established than those for ending a face-to-face interaction. In some cases, the patron will just close the chat while you are in the midst of ensuring that they got the information they needed. There are a couple of ways to manage this. Once you feel the transaction winding down, you could simply start with 'Before you sign off…' and then, in single-line transmissions, check on the patron's satisfaction with the information. If the patron's answer to 'Is there anything else I can help you with?' is 'Uh, no', then, virtually, we are in a bit of a pickle! Instead, try to elicit further information by asking a substantive question following the line of the patron's research. *Observe: IMRefDesk indicator F.* Using this technique over the course of the IM reference session is helpful because it encourages critical thinking and demonstrates that you are engaged with the patron.

Following up over the course of the entire transaction is another, and not mutually exclusive, option. This is also helpful in case technology fails us and our connection is somehow terminated. Your contact page comes in handy with the untimely terminations, too, since it provides a variety of ways to contact you again. Further, not all questions can best be answered over IM, so an e-mail or a telephone follow-up (or even a library visit!) would be an appropriate suggestion. *Observe: IMRefDesk indicator G.*

## Summary

Feeling comfortable with IM is essential to providing a successful IM reference transaction, so to get you off on the right, and comfortable, foot we provide a chart of IM general guidelines (Table 5.1). Working within these guidelines, and applying what we know about face-to-face reference, we are armed for success! Single-line transmissions keeping the patron apprised of the situation and engaged in the search work well. Adding more substance to traditional closed questions, such as 'Is this what you are looking for?', helps to ensure that we are best meeting our patrons' information needs. Remember, IM reference is reference just as face-to-face reference is!

6

# Managing patron expectations and staff attitudes

In any service industry, businesses devote significant consideration to their customers' needs: determining them, meeting them and anticipating them. Traditionally customer expectations, far trickier to predict since there are an infinite number of influencing factors, have often received disproportionately less consideration even though they are a considerable element in the customer service equation. This dynamic is changing in today's customer-centered marketplace. Libraries, as a service industry, mirror these practices and trends.

We know, and the literature corroborates, that many disparate factors shape patrons' expectations – from past service to attitudes toward technology, demographics and on and on.[1] And we know, too, that predicting, anticipating and building a structure to meet all expectations is impossible. Finally we know, as Jonathan Byrnes (2005) observes, that 'For nearly all customers, the most important need is to get what they plan on and expect.' Thus we must – especially given the technological shift that libraries face – consider our patrons' expectations and how they should shape our service.

Intimately connected to patron expectations, and far too often ignored, are staff attitudes. It is in the interplay between patron expectations and staff attitudes that we can build success or lapse into failure, often without understanding why. Analyzing patrons' expectations, staff attitudes and where they intersect is a vital exercise in building a strong and successful IM reference service!

## What do our patrons expect?

We need, just as in face-to-face reference, to be aware of potential expectations, err on the cautious but not-too-cautious side and take cues from our patrons. Patrons using reference services expect good service and an answer; not necessarily 'the' answer but an answer that helps them progress in their work/satisfy their curiosity. Using IM to provide reference adds an additional set of patron expectations. Let's discuss what they are and how we can meet them.

Patrons expect:

- immediate acknowledgement;
- indication of interest/attentive librarian;
- to be kept current while the librarian is working;
- time to respond/ask questions of librarian without feeling rushed;
- follow-up on resources and whether question has been answered;
- unscripted greeting and closing;
- rapport.

### *Immediate acknowledgement*

Immediately acknowledging patrons lets them know that they are connected and that it 'worked'! Acknowledgement can come in the form of canned messages, personal responses or a combination of these.

## *Indication of interest/attentive librarian*

Indicating interest in patrons' questions demonstrates that we are attentive and engaged. This is especially important because our body language and tone of voice are missing in the IM interaction.

## *To be kept current while the librarian is working*

Keeping patrons in the loop, explaining, even briefly, what you are doing in lieu of patrons watching you as you work, is necessary in IM reference. Even face to face it is good practice to explain what you are doing while you are working, rather than leaving patrons standing there in silence. Perhaps you are searching another database, perhaps it is taking longer than expected, perhaps there is another patron needing assistance simultaneously. Whatever the circumstances, simply keeping patrons apprised keeps them feeling listened to. Remember, the very nature of the IM interaction means that patrons will often be working on many other things while they're chatting with you. They often don't mind if the interaction takes a good deal of time to conclude; keeping them in the loop about your searching is more about remaining engaged with the user and imparting skills than it is necessarily about making sure they know you're still there.

## *Time to respond/ask questions of librarian without feeling rushed*

Some of the literature reports that patrons have said they feel the librarian is too busy to help them in face-to-face reference. Patrons report librarians looking engrossed in their work or uninterested in being at the reference desk. This issue carries additional import for IM reference since we are working in a setting where there is lag time and patrons cannot see us. It is incumbent upon us to encourage patrons to take the time they need to respond to our questions, to ask their own questions, to clarify their information needs and so on.

## *Follow-up on resources and whether question has been answered*

The visual clues available to us in face to face that indicate whether patrons feel they have the information they need – facial expression indicating understanding, gathering up belongings – are, we know, absent in virtual reference. As discussed in Chapter 5, an additional complication is the lack of cultural conventions regarding the appropriate way to end an IM conversation. Some patrons will stick around, engaging in 'traditional' farewells (thank you, goodbye, etc.). Others will simply disappear without so much as a word. Sometimes, that is just the way it is. To combat an abrupt interview ending, we should inquire as to the appropriateness of resources provided during the course of the entire interview and not just at the end. Further, we encourage you to follow up on patrons' comfort level using the suggested resources, since you cannot, obviously, walk around and see how the patron is doing in 15 minutes; and if patrons IM again 15 minutes later they very well may not get the same librarian on the other end of the line, and we would not want them to have to start from scratch. Just as we are in person, we are, in a sense, hamstrung on the follow-up: patrons leave the library just as patrons disconnect an IM session. All we can do is proactively check how useful suggested resources are.

## Unscripted greeting and closing

One could debate whether patrons *expect* or *prefer* an unscripted greeting or closing, but we feel that they are closer to expecting than preferring, so it made our list. Face-to-face interactions certainly don't rely on a scripted greeting and farewell; it wouldn't help make a patron feel welcome and comfortable. We think the same applies online. In fact, a scripted greeting or conclusion could amplify the feeling that the patron isn't talking to a 'real' person. But we recognize that some IM reference services are so heavily trafficked that scripted greetings and closings are a necessity. In that case, perhaps you could personalize a scripted greeting/closing by inserting patrons' names if you know them. If, however, your library experiences a moderate traffic level and you are able to include a personal touch, it goes a long way, as we have discussed earlier in the book.

The closing is a bit trickier, as mentioned in the previous section on follow-up. We should, as a practice, strive to include a substantive closing, inviting patrons back for further assistance by proclaiming our availability.

Use of canned communications is a contentious topic. Here we are interested in the greeting and closing, not the body of the transaction. For a solid primer on the pros and cons of canned communications, we suggest Straw (2006).

## Rapport

Building rapport in IM is an essential element in providing good service, since we do not have the benefit of smiles, nods or laughs as we do in face-to-face reference. Marie Radford (2003) lists recommendations for chat reference in a presentation she gave at a Virtual Reference Desk conference. All are relevant in building rapport, but we'd like to highlight a few: awareness of appropriate self-disclosure, humor and inclusion.

Self-disclosure on the part of both patron and librarian is a terrific way to establish rapport. Librarians should start all IM reference sessions with a most basic nod at self-disclosure – an introduction and a name to go with the 'face'. We recognize that not all librarians are comfortable sharing their names with patrons. If that is the case we recommend a consistent pseudonym – one that could be used to identify you if a patron comes to the library for a follow-up visit. Libraries will probably want to set up some kind of internal policy or guideline for the use of pseudonyms: they wouldn't be appropriate for all library environments. Following the introduction, on balance librarians should follow patrons' cues as to the amount of self-disclosure they wish to engage in. Again, librarians may be uncomfortable sharing their personal information. We have two suggestions. First, regardless, it is important, as Radford (ibid.) points out, to acknowledge patrons' self-disclosure. Second, we encourage you to think of self-disclosure in the most benign terms. More along the lines of 'Bear with me, I find this database useful but sometimes tricky to navigate', versus 'Bear with me, I'm an insomniac and didn't sleep much last night.' Radford modifies self-disclosure with 'appropriate', and we must be sure to keep that in mind. Just as the anonymity of IM lowers patron inhibitions, it might do the same for librarians. A good rule of thumb: write in IM only what you would say in person.

Humor lightens many situations. Remember, patrons may joke around to mask their discomfort or simply because they like to make jokes. Either way you should acknowledge humor to continue building rapport. With both self-disclosure and humor there is the potential for patrons and librarians to get carried away. If a patron seems to be going too far, simply acknowledge what was said and keep your focus on the search. As for librarians getting carried away, just remember to keep yourself in check, stay focused on the search and follow the patrons' cues.

Radford (ibid.) recommends inclusion, which she explains as 'use of we, let's, etc.'. This is an easy and effective method to use that has two main benefits. First, as we have been discussing, it helps build rapport since it shows that you value the patron's input and are working together. Second, it engages patrons and encourages them to work with you.

## What's the answer?

There are at times requests that we unfortunately cannot satisfy. It is vital that while responding and explaining the reasons why we cannot comply with a particular request, we remain willing to help, we indicate we are still available to help and we keep the tone light (unless of course it is an entirely inappropriate request, as is discussed below).

### *Patrons expecting you to do their work*

Certain scenarios warrant locating a specific answer for the patron. Perhaps it is your library's practice. Ready reference questions, too, might warrant a direct answer; we recommend in this case that you provide the name of the resource where you located said answer. What do we do if providing an answer is unreasonable, where patrons really do need to look at, read and evaluate sources on their own? This is stickier to deal with in IM: sometimes it might seem easier just to give an answer rather than guide a patron to a resource or teach a search strategy, because of all the typing. We encourage you to stick with your library's practice on this point and apply the same techniques you do in face-to-face reference: guide the patron in the search and map out a plan of action, suggest different resources to consult, use humor as appropriate (in IM indicate the humor with an emoticon when statements could be misunderstood) or give a resource you've located and explain how to leverage it further.

Caleb Tucker-Raymond (2007) insightfully illustrates a situation in which actually giving an answer is both appropriate and helpful: 'Since a previous relationship with a student in virtual reference usually does not exist, one of the best ways to establish one and build rapport is by answering the student's question. It is important to teach information literacy, it is important to affirm students' positive information-seeking behavior, but it is only possible if they trust us.' Many of us have been taught that giving patrons an answer is counterproductive; but keeping Tucker-Raymond's thoughts in mind, we can see that there are times when exercising our judgement and helping patrons create positive relationships and groundwork for the future.

## *Patrons expecting/requesting a service that your library does not provide*

A patron might request information or a service that your library does not provide. Here you have two options: you could politely tell the patron that you don't provide that service, and/or direct the patron to a library that does. A patron who is not part of your library's service population might request assistance. Your response options are similar: explain your service parameters and/or direct the patron to a library that can help.

### Patrons expecting 'too much' time

As discussed earlier in the book, some librarians are unsure how much time to spend IMing with a patron. This will differ by librarian and by library, but if you come to a point where you feel it necessary to end the IM session – whether it's because there are other patrons queued up or because you feel the user would benefit from looking at resources – encourage the patron to contact you again or come into the library.

### Inappropriate and lewd requests

Once you are confident that a patron is behaving inappropriately or being rude, try to redirect. If the patron is repeatedly inappropriate, simply disconnect. See Chapter 9 for more on this and on how to create policy to deal with inappropriate requests.

## Staff attitudes

Just as patron expectations of our IM reference services are influenced by a myriad of factors, so too are our staff attitudes. Clearly we all have our opinions about virtual reference and using IM as a delivery tool. As managers and co-workers we all have a responsibility to ensure that our staff provide effective, positive and consistent IM reference services. Whether staff do or do not favor IM reference, employing certain methods from the creation through to the implementation of the service helps to pave the way for good service.

Employment literature tells us, and workplace experience bears out, that when employers embark on new ventures, employees are happier and thus perform their new/additional responsibilities better if they are involved in the building process. Involvement in the creation process can be achieved in many ways – among the most effective are input into processes, understanding the project's purpose and how it fits into the big picture, and training. We recognize that these might not all be possible in your particular library's situation, but either way it helps to familiarize ourselves with the ideas. So let's look at how we can address these while building an IM reference service from both management and staff perspectives.

## *Input into processes*

### Management

Talk to those who know! Your staff will likely have opinions about virtual reference and IM. They are the front line, so ask them for their opinions about starting an IM reference service; solicit their suggestions on administering it; field their questions about performing IM reference, etc. However you choose to involve your staff, simply keeping them informed and listening to them will help build a successful service.

### Staff

Share your opinions with management and co-workers. Be frank about possibilities and concerns. Be open to new ideas.

## *Understanding purpose*

This occurs simultaneously with input into processes.

### Management

When you introduce the idea, frame IM reference as it relates to your reference services, to your library services and to the future of your library. Employees are far more likely to support IM reference when they understand its purpose: 'sharing the big-picture ideas with everyone who will listen... creates a stronger and more motivated work force, one willing to participate and share new ideas' (Casey and Stephens, 2007: 34). We all know that nothing exists in a vacuum.

### Staff

If you are curious about why IM reference, why now, why not chat or anything, and your management have not addressed the issue, ask. Now is the time.

## *Training*

### Management

Any new service offering requires training. We recommend making it mandatory so that the playing field is leveled and all staff are on the same page. If you can involve staff members in creating and/or delivering training, so much the better. Solicit training requests prior to building the training if possible. Follow-up training a few months into your new IM reference service would be helpful to iron out glitches and ensure your staff are happy. Training was discussed further in Chapter 4.

### Staff

Take advantage of the training to understand the ins and outs of IM and learn from your co-workers. Don't hesitate to ask for clarification or suggest areas for additional training.

## What are librarians thinking?

Some of us know from experience, some from the literature and some from thoughtful conjecture that, as with any new service, there are kinks to be worked out, reservations to be had. What, then, are the issues librarians think about when they consider provision of IM reference?

To explore what these issues are, we selected seven articles in which the authors either surveyed librarians or studied IM and chat transcripts. Librarians surveyed hailed from largely academic, but also public, corporate and government libraries. Publication dates range from 2002 to 2007, giving a sense of the evolution of ideas and technology both past and to come. Here, chronologically, are brief introductions to the articles.

- Fagan and Desai (2002) study IM and chat transcripts from their virtual reference service at Southern Illinois University and highlight effective strategies for communicating in a virtual environment. Salient for our discussion, though, is the summation Fagan and Desai give of their librarians' initial attitudes towards their IM reference service, which started in the summer of 2001.
- Kresh's (2002) comments on the informal survey she took of her Library of Congress colleagues are relevant for our purposes here. Her article provides an excellent overview of the development of virtual reference services and gives pointers on how to approach building such a service from lessons learned while the Library of Congress developed its online reference services.
- Foley (2002) discusses her library's (SUNY College at Buffalo) selection of IM software (AOL's IM), its implementation and patrons' and librarians' thoughts about the service.

- Janes and Hill (2002) focused on librarians' reflections on reference and how its practice is evolving, with particular attention to digital reference services. Their data come from two groups: a selected group of interviewees and a self-selected group of respondents from the DIG-REF list-serv.
- Connaway and Radford (2006) report as part of their larger study of virtual reference services sponsored by IMLS, Rutgers University and the OCLC. Connaway and Radford relay the results of two focus group interviews conducted with librarians at the 2005 Virtual Reference Desk Conference and the 2006 ALA Midwinter Conference.
- Steiner and Long (2007) asked academic librarians self-selected from five list-servs to respond to a survey that aimed to understand better librarian perceptions about IM and IM reference.
- Shrimplin and Hurst (2007) surveyed librarians from small, medium and large academic libraries to understand how they feel about virtual reference. The statements we include in our discussion are from the concourse of statements Shrimplin and Hurst included in their survey, not from the librarians surveyed. (Their article also contains a concise and clear explanation of Q methodology.)

Based on these articles we identified six primary issues that librarians are talking about. For each, we present ideas to help navigate the issues through listing 'What librarians are thinking about' and follow up with 'What librarians have said'. Librarians are concerned about:

- staffing;
- reference interviews;
- time;

- response quality;
- question type;
- worthwhile?

## *Staffing*

### What librarians are thinking about

- How do we integrate staffing the IM reference desk with the physical reference desk?
- Does the librarian providing face-to-face reference concurrently provide IM reference?
- How much additional time is required to staff the IM reference desk?
- How can we staff IM reference with a consortium?

### What librarians have said

- 'Some [librarians] objected to offering a new service when staffing shortages made it hard to staff the library's physical Information Desk' (Fagan and Desai, 2002: 122).
- 'What were major challenges in VRS? ... staffing...' (Connaway and Radford, 2006).
- 'Unable to staff via consortia' (Steiner and Long, 2007: 42).
- 'Finding the right staffing model to offer a sufficient level of service is a key consideration for smaller libraries' (ibid.: 43).

## *Reference interviews*

### What librarians are thinking about

- How can we effectively conduct reference interviews in IM?
- How do we interpret and convey non-verbal signals virtually?

- How do we keep the patron engaged while we determine the information need, and how much time do we spend doing so?

### What librarians have said

- '[Staff] felt the reference interview could not be conducted adequately in this medium and librarians would not be able to gauge the students' needs without the visual and aural cues to age, educational level, etc., that come with a face to face encounter' (Fagan and Desai, 2002: 123).
- 'The chat reference experience also seems superficial to some librarians and there are the usual worries about... the challenge of conducting the reference interview...' (Kresh, 2002: 25).
- 'Only occasionally is it necessary to engage in back in [*sic*] forth to get a good idea of the question' (Shrimplin and Hurst, 2007: 12).

## *Time*

### What librarians are thinking about

- How much time do we spend on an IM reference interaction?
- How much lag time is acceptable?
- How do typing skills factor into providing IM reference?

### What librarians have said

- 'Many [staff] simply felt it awkward and slow to answer questions by typing, copying, and pasting' (Fagan and Desai, 2002: 123).

- '...these concerns may be misplaced because few users complained that a librarian took too much time' (Foley, 2002: 43).
- 'Our respondents never mention the possibility that their users may already be aware that there is a potential time lag with digital reference services and instead assume that their patrons demand or expect immediate attention' (Janes and Hill, 2002: 62).
- 'Pressure for fast answers... Inadequate typing skills... Time-consuming method for responding to patrons (easier to use phone or face to face)' (Steiner and Long, 2007: 42).

## *Response quality*

### What librarians are thinking about

- How much information is ideal to give to the patron with respect to comprehension and retention?
- What level of detail strikes the best balance between treating a question fairly and going into enough depth?

### What librarians have said

- 'One concern that librarians commonly have is wondering if they will get the chance to explain the complexity of an informational problem to the patron' (Fagan and Desai, 2002: 152).
- 'The usual worries about... limiting the searches to the fast and easy (web content) and ignoring the research oriented and comprehensive (all the analog stuff)' (Kresh, 2002: 25).

- 'I have found myself debating whether to tell someone how to do something online, which would mean a lot of typing, or just pushing the results of what I've done for them' (Shrimplin and Hurst, 2007: 11).

## Question type

### What librarians are thinking about

- How will the nature of IM shape reference questions?

### What librarians have said

- 'They expressed greater satisfaction with VRS than with face-to-face reference encounters because they are asked fewer directional and more diverse, challenging questions' (Connaway and Radford, 2006).
- 'Questions are directional not reference oriented' (Steiner and Long, 2007: 42).
- 'Quick factual questions are the best because we don't have the body; anything that has depth should be a consultation' (Shrimplin and Hurst, 2007: 12).

## Worthwhile?

### What librarians are thinking about

- How does IM reference enhance our services?
- How can we justify the additional workload?

### What librarians have said

- 'Many librarians are concerned about the lack of efficiency and value of providing IM or chat reference.

The lack of questions during slow periods leads some librarians to feel these services are a waste of time... Another general concern about IM and chat is the ability to be available when the service is most needed' (Steiner and Long, 2007: 43).

- 'For all the hype about reaching out in extraordinary ways and in unusual times, virtual reference fails our users. It doesn't meet their information needs efficiently, and it doesn't deepen their research capabilities' (Shrimplin and Hurst, 2007: 12).
- 'I have absolutely no regrets about enhancing our reference services through chat' (ibid.: 13).

Among other concerns librarians raised were accessibility and logs. Over the evolution of IM reference these issues have become less and less of a worry. Please see Chapter 4 for a discussion of logs.

## Summary

Among patrons, expectations about IM reference differ. While it may not be possible for us always to know what those expectations are, awareness of potential expectations helps us anticipate and tailor our IM reference service accordingly. Don't expect to meet them all – that's okay! Staff attitudes are a corollary to patron expectations, and we can see from the literature that attitudes towards virtual and IM reference range across the spectrum. So, once again, there is no quick fix! But, again, awareness of the issues that librarians are thinking about with regard to virtual and IM reference helps us build morale and a strong service.

## Note

1. We recommend Lorri Mon (2006) to explore the intricacies of user perceptions and expectations.

7

# Evaluating/updating service

> Before beginning an assessment project, develop a clear statement of the specific questions you want to answer, the measurable data needed to answer your questions, and the performance or quality standards you will use to measure your success. Next, choose assessment tools that are relevant to your stated goals. Modify existing tools to meet your needs, and always pretest your tool on a small representative sample of data or subjects. Finally, to have greater confidence in the validity of your results, use more than one assessment tool. (American Library Association, 2007)

Traditionally, reference has proven challenging to evaluate because of the evanescence of the reference transaction. A benefit of virtual reference is the automatically captured data each virtual transaction generates. IM reference provides transcripts in the form of logs, which can be phenomenally useful for evaluative purposes since they afford us a second (and third and fourth) look at a given reference session and allow us to reflect on our service. This reflection provides us with more substantive tools for evaluating IM reference, which then enable us to enhance our service.

Program evaluation can indeed be overwhelming! There are many data, there are many angles from which to view your data and there are a variety of goals you may be working towards. Two key pieces of advice: stay focused, and gather only data you will use. If, upon reviewing your data, you discover an interesting trend that you hadn't anticipated and thus hadn't included in your evaluation plan, save it for your next evaluation. If you have a tendency to operate on the 'more is better' premise with data gathering, curb your enthusiasm. Think about it in terms of your patrons: do not waste their time gathering data you will not use.

Measuring success is a paramount consideration in an evaluation. Determine in advance of your evaluation, and ideally in advance of implementing your service (McClure et al., 2002: 6), what performance levels will indicate success for your IM reference service. This way you are not biased by your actual performance, nor are your expectations biased. Currently, user satisfaction for virtual reference is typically measured by patrons' willingness to use your service again. This is true for most service industries. According to Jonathan Byrnes (2005), 'Customer service is what the customer perceives and remembers. The acid test of customer service is the customer's future behavior.' Since patrons are not necessarily assured they will IM the same librarian, however, Jeffrey Pomerantz (2008: 17, emphasis in original) qualifies this satisfaction measure: 'Willingness to return is an appropriate metric of user satisfaction for online reference, but it must be modified to mean willingness to return to submit another question to the same *service*.' Exit surveys, analysis of log data and/or patron indication will yield this desired and useful statistic.

## Gathering data

Which begs the question, then, how do you gather data? Here is a list of possibilities:

- logs/transcripts;
- patron surveys – online and written;
- librarian surveys – online and written;
- interviews;
- focus groups.

Privacy is an issue with data gathering. If you plan on using logs and transcripts, you'll want to be sure it is part of your policy statement so patrons are aware of this. Another interesting issue is the 'exit' survey often conducted just after a patron signs off. While convenient in terms of having patrons' attention, the issue has been raised (for example Mon, 2006; Pomerantz, 2008) that the ideal time to ask patrons about their satisfaction with the reference session would be after they have had time to evaluate the resources received. To do this, because of privacy issues, librarians would need to ask patrons for e-mail addresses to follow up and then manually send a follow-up e-mail questionnaire. Therein lies the rub! Not only does it create more work for librarians, but also we may have lost our 'captive' audience.

## Let's evaluate

In their book *Starting and Operating Live Virtual Reference Services*, Meola and Stormont (2002: 145–51) lay out a clear and concise evaluation plan that could be used either alone or as the foundation for a more extensive effort:

- revisit your vision;
- evaluate software;
- assess staffing;
- review questions;
- analyze answers;
- produce a report.

## Revisit your vision

As with any evaluation effort, at the outset it is good practice to remind ourselves of the vision we started with for our IM reference service – good practice because it refocuses us on the purpose of IM reference, which may get lost in the day-to-day practice and logistics, and it enables us to shape our evaluation effort to achieve that vision. Decide upon the best way to evaluate how well you have met your vision. The vital next step is setting 'a performance standard for what constitutes success in the area in which you want to evaluate' (ibid.: 146). Janes (2003: 180) echoes this instruction: 'It's nice to be able to say that you answer 65 percent of your questions within 48 hours or that 72 percent of people would recommend your service to others, but without standards or targets to compare those figures to, they don't mean much.' Be sure that the standards/targets you come up with are both realistic and productive, so that you have a fair shot at reaching them and you are truly assessing your service.

## Evaluate software

We all know how easy it is to take our technology for granted until something goes awry. We also know how frustrating it is when we are retrieving an article from a database or even buying books online and there is a glitch in the software.

Meola and Stormont (2002) advocate preventive care: make sure your software is working as it should and that the features are functioning as promised. Check, too, how the software is affecting your hardware. Once we promise to provide IM reference, we need to be sure we are up and running at the most base level or we will alienate potential patrons. Keeping our software healthy is an easy part of that process!

## Assess staffing

As we discuss in Chapters 6 and 9, staffing is a key issue for IM reference services. Librarians are thinking about their workload, about staffing both face-to-face and IM reference and whether they can provide IM reference when their patrons need the service. Meola and Stormont (ibid.: 147) advise us to consider all these issues when we assess staffing. Further, they ask 'How does the staff feel about the service? Are they enthusiastic or are they grumbling about it behind the project coordinator's back?' We all have elements of our jobs that we prefer and go about readily and elements that we don't particularly care for and go about grudgingly. Nothing wrong with that! It does, however, become a problem if it affects the quality of service. Regularly ask your librarians how they feel about your IM reference service and, if there is cause for concern, observe a bit. Work with those librarians whose strengths may lie elsewhere and determine an appropriate course of action. A happy librarian provides quality service!

## Review questions

With your question review, you are basically looking for how many, what type and received when. All of which are interesting questions in and of themselves, but for a purposeful evaluation you must have a target in mind prior to reviewing your questions with which to compare your results. Otherwise you have thought-provoking data and little else.

- *How many*: when looking at how many questions you've received, you'll want to compare to the number of face-to-face, e-mail and phone questions as well as to prior months' (weeks', years') numbers.
- *Type*: in terms of type of questions, Meola and Stormont (ibid.: 149) ask us to consider if 'there are certain kinds of questions... that are outnumbering other questions'; and if so, consider adding them to an FAQ list. Perhaps you could create workshops based upon topics/questions that arise repeatedly.
- *Time*: what time your IM service receives questions helps you play with staffing levels to ensure the most comprehensive and useful coverage.

## Analyze answers

We've all done it: continued working on a reference question after the patron has walked away, determined to find another, a better, a different answer! Transcripts of our IM reference sessions now allow us to review the answers we give. This is important not because we are curious folk, but because quality control is always a good thing. Meola and Stormont (ibid.) warn us not to spend a disproportionate amount of time poring over transcripts, but instead to skim to two ends:

- try to glance at the transcripts at least once a week and look for warning signs – questions that are not being answered, a pattern of incomplete answers, unhappy patron responses;
- check to see that the agreed-upon live virtual reference policies are being followed.

When time allows, we encourage you to take some time to read and analyze properly the answers your librarians are giving, for both learning and training purposes (for more on training see Chapter 4). Here, as with question review, we must have a standard/target, as Pomerantz (2008: 16) elaborates: 'The trick to conducting content analysis on reference transcripts, however, is rigorously defining what constitutes an accurate and complete answer or an instance of instruction or an expression of thanks... For the analysis to be reliable, the scopes of the categories used to code content must be clear.' If you find that your categories are effective, then by all means stick with them. If, however, you find you are having difficulties categorizing answers, play with your categorization to make the most of your analyses.

## *Produce a report*

Once you gather and analyze all of your data it is good practice to produce a report. Perhaps you have to present your findings to stakeholders or you have to convince your director that launching IM reference was indeed a good idea, or perhaps you just want the information for historical purposes. The idea is that, regardless of purpose, it is best to capture the information and ideas now. Again we advise focus: include in your report information that is useful, not just interesting; information that will help you make decisions which will enhance your service. And be sure that your report is as objective as possible, presenting an unbiased view of your IM reference service.

Finally, we would be remiss if we did not direct you to one of the seminal works in evaluating digital reference: McClure et al. (2002: iv) 'describe specific techniques, statistics, and measures that could be used to assess digital reference services'. Their manual is comprehensive and immeasurably helpful.

## Summary

Evaluating your IM reference service will help you stay fresh and build success! Always remember to stay focused, gather only the data you will use and thoughtfully assess your service. Don't box yourself in! Perhaps it's time for a different staffing model. Or perhaps your evaluation reveals that Sunday afternoons are a high-traffic time. Whatever your data reveal, be mindful and open to adjusting your IM reference service accordingly. Remember, there is no one recipe for success!

8

# Taking your service to the next level: widgets, enterprise IM and collaborative IM

This book has so far been about IM reference at its most basic. We want, primarily, to provide a starting point for libraries considering an IM reference service and needing the bare-bones information to get their services going. Our central message has been that IM is an exceedingly easy way to extend your reference services. Download some simple software, make some basic decisions about how to handle the workflow, get the word out and you've got a service ready to go!

Already have an IM reference service going? Want to extend your service by adding widgets to your site? Interested in running your own IM server? Intrigued by collaborative IM? In this chapter, we'll examine IM beyond the basics.

## The wonderful world of widgets

Not so very long ago, placing an IM 'widget' on your library's website was the very cutting edge of IM reference service. By now, it has become almost *de rigueur.* IM widgets have become popular because they are so incredibly easy to implement and deliver such dramatic results!

## What is a 'widget'?

'Widget' is the term of art for a chunk of code that can be embedded in a standard HTML webpage to bring in content from a third party. Usually, widgets employ Adobe Flash, DHTML and/or JavaScript to allow for interactivity. Put another way, widgets are pieces of reusable code, designed to be easy for relatively non-technical people to embed in webpages for the purpose of adding functionality and/or content from a third party to their sites.

IM widgets allow you to add a 'chatbox' to your website by taking a snippet of code and inserting it into your webpage. As we'll discuss below, this allows patrons to chat with you via IM anonymously and without having IM software installed on their computers.

The IM widget 'market' is an increasingly crowded one and changing all the time. Figure 8.1 features some of the major players in the world of widgets as of this writing. We've provided an image of a typical widget from each of these providers; remember, though, that some offer significant opportunity for formatting the widget to your particular taste. We have also provided some background information on each of the widgets, along with basic information about the options for customization and methods of branding employed by each of the providers.

## How do you get a widget?

Building a widget is easy. Remember, the whole *point* of widgets is to provide non-technical people with an easy way to do something that in the past would have required some programming chaps.

The process of obtaining a widget will be some variation of the following.

**Figure 8.1** **Popular widgets and their features**

| **Widget** | **Description** | **Options** | **Branding** |
|---|---|---|---|
| MeeboMe<br>www.meebome.com<br><br> | Currently most commonly used widget<br>Probably around to stay, Google having purchased Meebo not long ago<br>Uses Jabber | Size labels<br>Choose from pre-set color schemes | 'get meebo' logo in corner |
| Hab.la<br>http://hab.la<br>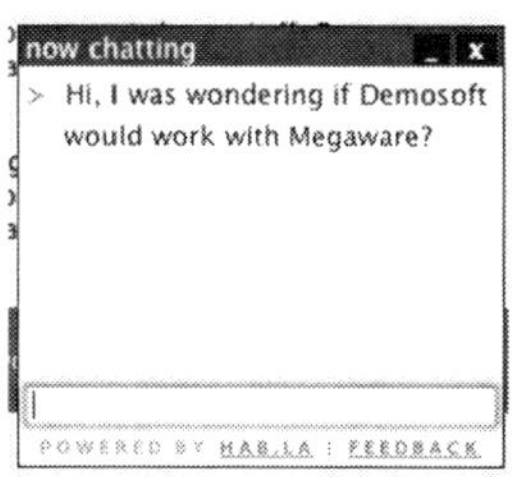<br> | Uses Jabber protocol<br>Unique in that it allows a chat to 'follow' patrons across pages<br>Currently can only support 5 chats simultaneously | None | 'Powered by HAB.LA' link |
| Plugoo<br>www.plugoo.com<br><br> | Forwards chat requests to an existing IM account – e.g. you give it your Yahoo! user name and it forwards chats to your Yahoo! account | Labels<br>Size<br>Colors<br>Messages | 'Get your Plugoo' button on bottom<br>Logo can be removed for $4.99/month subscription fee |

**Figure 8.1** **Popular widgets and their features (*Cont'd*)**

| Widget | Description | Options | Branding |
|---|---|---|---|
| Chatango http://chatango.com 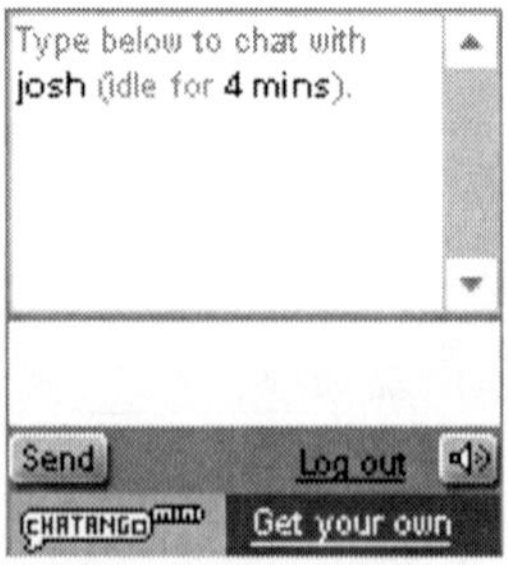  | Users must sign in to the Chatango website and monitor chats from there This makes Chatango a poor choice for IM reference, in our opinion | None | Chatango logo and 'get your own' link |
| LibraryH3lp http://libraryh3lp.blogspot .com/   | Discussed in detail later in this chapter Exciting project designed to support collaborative IM for libraries, started by a librarian Designed by a librarian for libraries Uses Jabber | Fully customizable | None |

- Sign up at site of the widget provider – this usually involves providing some basic information like user name and e-mail address.
- Customize your widget – most widget providers will allow you to do some basic customization of colors, sizes, etc.
- Copy the code generated by the website.
- Paste it into your website wherever you'd like your chat widget to appear.

We'll illustrate the process of obtaining a widget using the MeeboMe widget. MeeboMe is just one of the widgets available, and the steps for getting other widgets might be slightly different. This is meant to give you a general idea of the process.

- Visit site and customize widget: MeeboMe lets you choose colors, size and labels (Figure 8.2).
- Create account or add account information. MeeboMe requires the use of a Meebo account (Figure 8.3).
- Copy the code from the site (Figure 8.4).

In the example above, the code generated was this little snippet:

```
<!-- Beginning of meebo me widget code.
Want to talk with visitors on your page?
Go to http://www.meebome.com/ and get your widget! -->
<embed src="http://widget.meebo.com/mm.swf?codedeleted"
type="application/x-shockwave-flash" wmode="transparent"
width="190" height="275"></embed>
```

When Rachel pasted it into her website she got the widget shown in Figure 8.5.

## *OK, I have the widget, now how do I chat using it?*

There isn't one simple answer to this question, sadly. Each widget has its own quirks. Some integrate into any IM client, some can be added as an account on any client that supports the Jabber/XMPP protocol (like Pidgin, Adium, Trillian Pro or Meebo) and others expect you to monitor the chat via a web browser.

Though we try to be 'product neutral' in this book, not strongly advocating the use of one tool over another nor

**Figure 8.2** Visit site and customize widget

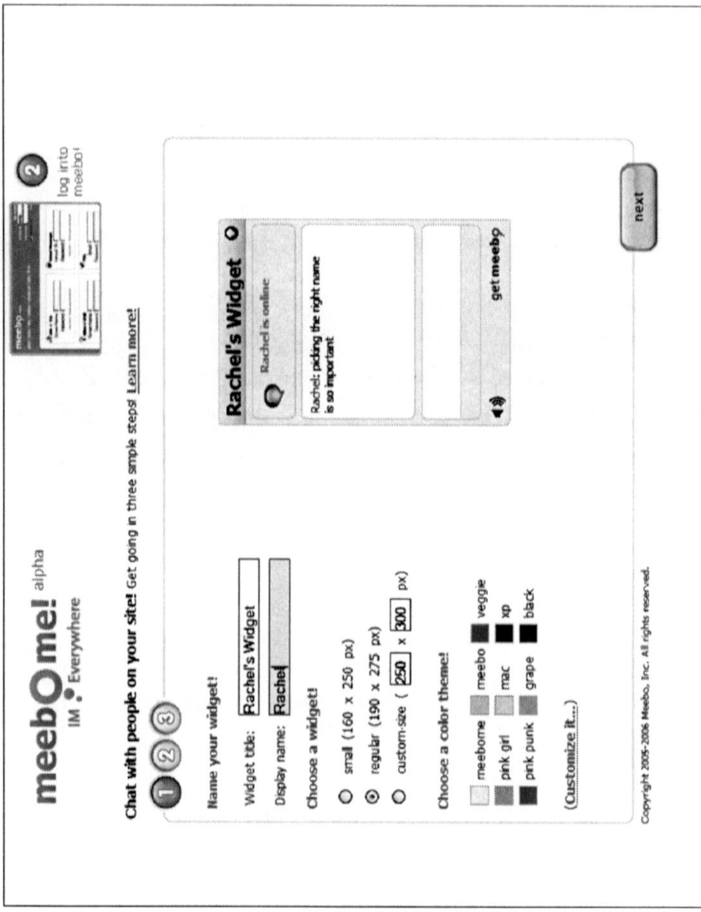

**Figure 8.3** Create account or add account information

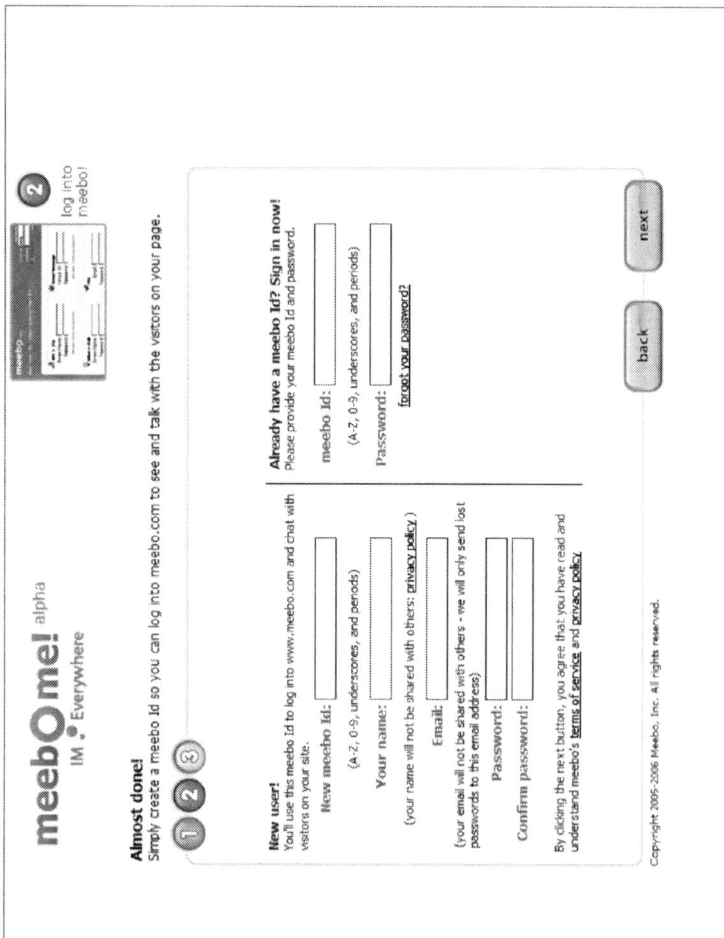

**Figure 8.4** Copy the code from the site

**Figure 8.5** Example of a widget

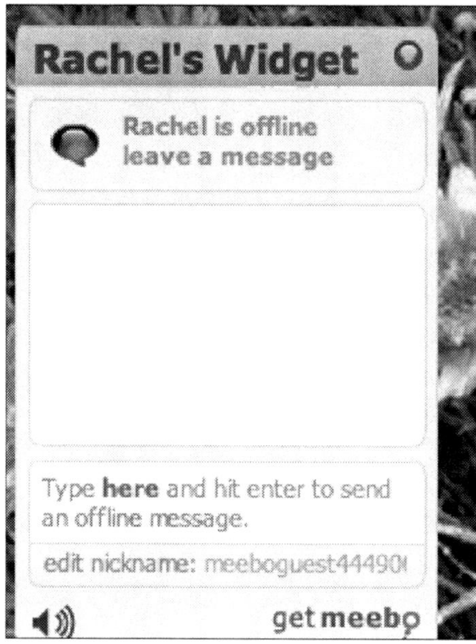


spending too much time on any particular tool, especially because these things change so quickly, we are going to take a moment to address the particular case of using the MeeboMe widget with the Pidgin client. This is a popular widget/client combination and demonstrates some of the 'tricks' that make this topic suitable for the 'advanced' section of this book.

MeeboMe uses the Jabber/XMPP protocol, which is terrific because it means that it can be used with any client that supports Jabber. Unfortunately, MeeboMe isn't really designed to do the kinds of things we're asking it to do in libraries, so there are some tricks that must be employed! First, when you sign up for your MeeboMe widget, you'll see that the site refers you to the Meebo site to use your widget. This makes sense because, naturally, Meebo would like you to use the Meebo client with its widget. It is just like when you create your AOL or Yahoo! account and are directed to download their software. You know now, after reading this book, that it's not necessary to use their software to use their protocols. The same thing is true of your MeeboMe widget and Meebo. Meebo does provide some limited help for getting the account set up in your Jabber client – a short link at the end of its help screens and a screenshot showing where the various settings should go.

The basic set-up in your Jabber client is:

Protocol: Jabber/XMPP
Screen name: The name of your widget
Server: meebo.org
Resource: Pidgin.

Happily, this small bit of help is truly all you need to start answering widget questions from your desktop client. Perfect, right? Not exactly. The first thing you'll notice after you do this is that you start getting authorization request after authorization request from the widget. You are getting a buddy authorization request from everyone who visits the page with the widget on it! If you've placed the widget on your homepage (and why wouldn't you?), you're going to be inundated with requests. This is where Pidgin comes in. If you're using Pidgin, you can simply install the very clever Pidgin4Lib plug-in (www.lib.unc.edu/reference/eref/pidgin/meebomewidget.html) and you won't be bothered by those authorization requests any more!

Nothing too tricky here, but enough to take it out of the realm of 'straightforward'. Table 8.1 gives a quick overview of some popular widgets and how to use them.

**Table 8.1** **How to use some popular widgets**

| | |
|---|---|
| MeeboMe | On the Meebo website (using the Meebo client) or via a desktop XMPP client |
| Chatango | Via the Chatango website; you must be signed into a web browser to monitor it |
| Plugoo | Forwards messages to whichever IM client you specify |
| Hab.la | Via an XMPP client |
| LibraryH3lp | Via an XMPP client |

## Widget advantages

There are a number of benefits to using widgets on your webpages:

- anonymity;
- convenience;
- visibility;
- access;
- point-of-need service.

### *Anonymity*

One of the biggest issues for librarians using IM for reference services is the unfortunate fact that it is difficult to provide a meaningfully private way to chat using the traditional commercial IM products. Patrons using an IM widget on your website enjoy a very high degree of privacy because they are completely anonymous in their chat with you. The widget assigns them an automatic ID that has nothing to do with their identity and requests the chat with you using that anonymous ID. The ability to offer very private chat is, to our way of thinking, a powerful argument for using an IM widget.

### Convenience

Traditionally, if a patron wanted to chat with you they would need to have an IM account themselves. As we've discussed, a great number of your patrons will have one of these accounts, but not all. Most will not be interested in creating an account and downloading software just so that they can chat with their librarian. Even those who have IM accounts would need to be using a computer that had the IM software installed and configured to access their accounts. By adding a widget to your page, you're providing a way for patrons to reach you when they are not signed into an IM account – either because they don't have one or because they simply aren't using it at the time.

### Visibility

Seeing an active chatbox on your library's website is a much more immediate call to action than a link that says 'Ask a librarian' or 'IM a librarian'. Adding the chatbox will immediately increase the visibility of your service.

### Access

Adding an IM widget to your webpages makes the service available to everyone, not just people who use IM.

### Point-of-need service

Not only does the IM widget make your service more visible, but it has the potential to put your service where your users need it most. Are there areas of your website where people get confused? Put an IM widget there! Put an IM widget on your help pages. David Lee King at Topeka & Shawnee County Public Library writes about adding an IM widget in the catalog when patrons run a search that gets no results. You can be very creative about where you place these widgets!

In the narrative below, Kate Gronemyer from the Oregon State University Cascades Library describes how adding a chat widget to their library webpages transformed her library's IM reference service.

> Sometimes it's good to be in a small library. Deciding to implement instant messenger reference service was as simple as, well, deciding to do it. I thought a little about what might happen if IM reference was so popular that I was chained to my desk, chatting the day away, but decided to take my chances and signed up for IM accounts with AIM, Y!M, MSN Messenger and ICQ. I then set up a Trillian account so I could monitor them all from a single interface. I added our screen names to the library's 'contact us' webpage, put them in the brochure we give every student in orientation, posted them near every computer in our computer lab and talked up IM when I taught classes. Then I braced myself for the flood of chatting... that never came. I can count the number of student questions I've had over IM on one hand.
>
> So was creating IM reference a total waste of time? Not in my book. First of all, it didn't take very much time and we didn't have to pay any fees, subscriptions, etc. I have it set to log me in automatically so I don't have to remember to open it up in the morning, and it notices when I'm away from my computer, too. I do use it fairly regularly to chat with colleagues. A few pieces of advice for someone just starting out: I wouldn't bother with the ICQ and MSN accounts. If students ask for them you could always add them later, but they seem to be far less

popular than AIM and Y!M. Also, Yahoo! Instant Messenger allows a few more characters in a screen name than AOL Instant Messenger (16 characters), so if you want to use the same name in both systems you will need to make it no longer than 16 characters.

In fall 2006 I added a Meebo widget to our page so that folks could ask questions without signing into (or even having) any type of instant messenger account. The widget has proven to be more popular than our other IM reference services. This may be because we have mostly non-traditional (i.e. older than average) students who aren't using IM in their regular lives, but it's also just easier. We advertise it as 'No signup, no login, no problem!' The service isn't perfect; I have to remember to log in and also to change my status to 'away' if I'm leaving my desk, and there are some other features (like chat logging or sending live URLs) I'm hoping they will add in the future, but I love it anyway. I tend to get a lot of repeat business on the Meebo widget. When students (or faculty) use it once, they seem likely to use it again. It has also been a first-time chatting experience for some students and faculty members. Occasionally I end up using the phone or e-mail to answer questions that started as a chat, but often I can send a link or two that are exactly what the person was looking for and they're always thrilled. (Kate Gronemyer, Oregon State University Cascades Library)

## Issues/problems with widgets

Widgets are undoubtedly a benefit to your IM reference service but they aren't without their issues, such as:

- integration with traditional IM clients;
- usability;

- advertisements/branding;
- relying on a third party.

## Integration with traditional IM clients

As we discussed above, IM widgets don't always 'play nice' with the IM software you're already using.

## Usability

One of the biggest issues with most chat widgets is that the user must stay on the current page in order for the chat to continue. The dynamically generated user name associated with the loading of the page vanishes once they navigate away. You can imagine how often chats are 'lost' because the patron changes pages. After all, if the patron is asking you for help with a library question they are likely doing something else that involves navigating to different webpages. Libraries are handling this in a couple of ways.

- Provide a link to the patron to 'pop' the chat out of the page, using JavaScript.
- Replace the live chat window with an *image* of a chat window; when the patron clicks on it, use JavaScript to open a new window with the actual chat in it (see Figure 8.6). We highly recommend this system: it requires nothing from the patron but that they click on the chatbox. Because it doesn't require the user to notice the 'pop-up' link or take any additional action, it is the most reliable method.

Some widgets, like hab.la, are beginning to address this problem with technology that allows the widget to 'follow' the patron from screen to screen. This is a most welcome advance, and we will not be at all surprised if this is where all of the widgets go in the coming years.

**Figure 8.6** Oregon State University Libraries' chatbox image

```
<!-- ask your librarian -->
<div style="background: transparent
url(http://osulibrary.oregonstate.edu/
images/chatbox.jpg) repeat scroll 0%; -moz-background-clip:
-moz-initial; -moz-background-origin: -moz-initial; -moz-
background-inline-policy: -moz-initial;" id="ask">
<a href="javascript:launch_meebome('2')"></a>
```

### Advertisements/branding

At a minimum, unless you use the LibraryH3lp widget or pay for premium service, your widget will contain some sort of text branding it as a 'Meebo' widget or a 'Plugoo' widget. After all, these firms are providing these snippets of code primarily as a way to get people to use their services. Some libraries will have a difficult time accommodating such obvious branding on their homepages. To our way of thinking, we have patrons using clearly branded products – from Elsevier, Ebsco, CSA and the rest – all the time. This isn't any different, but it does give some librarians pause as it is usually featured so prominently on the library's website.

### Reliance on a third party

Relying on a third party that makes no warranties to you for such a core service is risky. What if the MeeboMe widget isn't working for a day because the Meebo servers are having problems? What if Plugoo stops providing the service? This is a different model for working with third parties than we're accustomed to in libraries, where we typically purchase services from third parties and, with that purchase, get some guarantee that the service will continue to exist and work the way we expect it to.

## XMPP, enterprise IM, collaborative IM and the future of IM reference

When libraries first started offering IM reference services it was almost by following the same basic steps we discussed in Chapter 4. It was just a way of extending reference service without a lot of overhead. IM was in no way able to replace or replicate the features of the big virtual reference software programs many libraries use. At the time of writing this is still largely true, but it's changing. One thing that the big chat reference programs have been able to offer is the ability to do truly collaborative service – to create a queue of librarians and route the question to the right one. IM was never designed to do that. But where there is a need, products arise to fill it. We'll use the rest of this chapter to look at enterprise IM, the XMPP protocol, collaborative IM and the future of IM reference.

## Enterprise IM

Caleb Tucker-Raymond, the project coordinator of Oregon's state-wide virtual reference service, L-Net, has spent a lot of time in the last couple of years thinking about enterprise IM. He had a vision of improving collaborative virtual reference service by using IM, but couldn't find any easy solutions when he started searching. Things have changed a lot in that time; there are now some truly viable options out there for libraries interested in using IM collaboratively. For now, we're going to allow Caleb to introduce the topic of enterprise IM. Later we'll build on Caleb's introduction and talk about an exciting project out of the University of North Carolina called LibraryH3lp.

### *XMPP and enterprise IM: an introduction by Caleb Tucker-Raymond*

A patron approaches the reference desk in a small branch library at a large university. She wants a book about instant messaging reference, but the catalog shows the book is deep in the basement of the main library. Before sending the patron over, the librarian quickly messages the desk at the main library with the call number and the patron's barcode to have the book retrieved before the patron gets there.

A busy 'information commons' has librarians and IT staff together answering reference questions and helping with computer problems. When both people are busy and there's an obvious need for more help, staff simply broadcast an IM to everyone in the back – 'someone come out and help' – and someone does come.

A reference librarian receives a tentative instant message from a screen name she doesn't recognize, 'hello?'. As she would for any other patron, she introduces herself and begins a reference interview. The patron clarifies what he wants: sex. The librarian reacts by disconnecting and blocking the patron. Later, he returns with another screen name and asks for the same thing. The librarian can either accept sexual harassment or make another screen name.

All of these things might happen at a library using a commercial instant messaging service to communicate, and some of them might just as easily happen with a phone call. But phones lack the convenience of carrying written information, and commercial instant messaging services lack the privacy and control that a local instant messaging service would provide.

Enterprise instant messaging (EIM) is industry jargon for just that kind of local instant messaging service. Organizations with an organic or imposed culture of IM use have recognized that if their members are going to use IM, the organization is better off if it takes control of its IM service.

In hospitals and health agencies, the Health Insurance Portability and Accounting Act (HIPAA) strictly controls what kinds of health information can be shared within and without the organization. In response to several capitalist scandals, laws such as the Sarbanes-Oxley Act of 2002 require publicly traded companies to report and archive financial information strictly for auditing.

Many institutions protect their internal network security by using firewalls to block traffic on 'unneccessary' TCP/IP ports, including the ones that commercial IM services use.

Any company that depends on non-disclosure for its competitive edge does not want to share internal secrets with outside companies through a commercial instant messaging service. Imagine employees at Yahoo! using AOL Instant Messenger to discuss a new business strategy.

Institutions that want to make sure employees follow all behavior policies might want to filter dirty words on instant messaging, and they certainly would want to be able to track down the source of a sexual harassment complaint.

Enterprise IM is used whenever an organization wants to control the instant messaging service its members use – whether for privacy, auditing, security, confidentiality or to be able to enforce internal policies.

Privacy, in particular, is of concern to libraries. In recent years it has made sense for libraries to join the networks that patrons use, including social networking sites and instant messaging services. These services are controlled by commercial enterprises and, besides talking about it to them, there is not much libraries can do about patron privacy in these environments. Surely institutions have a greater responsibility to protect privacy than individuals do, and libraries' responsibility is to keep transactions with patrons confidential except when required by law and, increasingly, except when patrons wish explicitly to share them with others. It is reasonable for libraries to join commercial networks as an extension of the library's services in order to connect with patrons who have chosen to use those networks, but it is irresponsible to base entire services on them when we have other choices.

The most common software platform for enterprise IM is Jabber, an open source instant messaging platform developed in 1998 and later standardized as XMPP (Extensible Messaging and Presence Protocol). Three things distinguish Jabber/ XMPP (www.xmpp.org/about/) from other instant messaging services: it is open, it is decentralized and it is extensible.

Jabber is open in that the software itself is developed as an open source server for instant messaging. In 2002 the XMPP protocol was formally adopted by the Internet Engineering Task Force, an internet standards organization (www.xmpp .org/about/history.shtml). In addition to Jabber being available as an open source tool, having XMPP as a standard protocol makes it possible to create other tools based on the same protocol, such as 'transports' or gateways to connect XMPP services to other types of communication protocols.

Gateways for some XMPP servers exist for commercial IM networks like AIM, Yahoo! Messenger, MSN Messenger, voice over IP and ICQ, and so long as there's interest in the developer community, XMPP transports may exist for sending and receiving text messages (SMS), RSS feeds, e-mail and any kind of communication you can think of.

XMPP IM services are decentralized in the same way that e-mail services are. On a commercial instant messaging service, every session is initiated through a central server. A user on one instant messaging service generally cannot communicate with users on another instant messaging service.

Compare this to how e-mail services are structured today. Anyone with an e-mail account can send a message to anyone else with an e-mail account, no matter where both of those two people hold their accounts, because e-mail servers all share a common protocol, SMTP (Simple Messaging and

Transfer Protocol). XMPP services are structured similarly. Depending on the server settings, a person using one XMPP service can IM with a person using another XMPP service. In theory, every individual who runs an e-mail server might eventually want to run an instant messaging server as well.

XMPP is not actually based on the SMTP protocol, however, and has one major difference. SMTP does not require senders to verify their identity, in the same way that you can put any fake return address on a letter you send through the mail. SMTP makes anonymous communication easy, which is important for free speech, but the protocol has also opened the floodgates for unsolicited spam e-mail. XMPP has a built-in control to require that the receiver authorizes the receipt of the message from the sender, which prevents spim, or unsolicited IM spam.

The X in XMPP is for 'Extensible'. (As library professionals, we know that this word starts with E, but never mind.) XMPP was inspired by XML, eXtensible Markup Language, which, rather than being a standard for encoding information, is a standard for creating standards. The bones of what is encoded in the XMPP standard are very much what you'd expect in an instant messaging service: who sent the message, who was it to, when was it sent and what was the message itself? Beyond that, anyone can add information to send along with the messages, such as encryption keys, images and other documents as part of the message, and simple messages like 'you've got mail'.

Openness, decentralization and extensibility have allowed people to create their own tools and services based on the XMPP protocol. The two best known in libraries, perhaps, are gTalk and Meebo. gTalk is Google's instant messaging service and is available to everyone with a Gmail account. gTalk also includes mail notification for Gmail, and voice over IP for people with headsets connected to their computers. Meebo is a web-based IM aggregator that allows people to monitor their IM accounts from multiple services at the same time. The core of Meebo's service is an XMPP account, and the company has built on the popular MeeboMe widget, which connects an anonymous web user to your XMPP account with Meebo, and also allows selected developers to extend Meebo's web-based platform.

Libraries can make use of XMPP services in other ways, as well. A simple server on a local network can ensure confidentiality when sending patrons' barcodes between service points; clever software can allow the broadcast of a message to a whole group; and servers can keep records of transactions for statistics and to enforce policies against the abuse of the service. By making use of 'transports' to commercial IM services, network personnel can make sure unwanted viruses are stopped before they reach staff computers.

These are all ways for libraries to use enterprise IM to control IM usage in the library, which is progressive in that it might help ensure patron privacy, but regressive in that it might encourage monitoring of staff activities. Besides the purposes of privacy and control, libraries may also want to use enterprise IM to expand their current services.

For example, a central XMPP server could manage virtual reference and telephone service on a local voice-over-IP network, letting a reference call center handle both IM and telephone reference without having to assign different personnel to different responsibilities. Enterprise IM can be the core of a collaborative virtual reference service, if the extensible nature of XMPP is expanded to include a routing service to send instant messages to the next available librarian. An XMPP gateway to a text messaging/SMS service could let librarians send text messages to patrons using mobile devices without having to use an awkward mobile device themselves.

Not every library has its own e-mail server today, with this duty usually relegated to a parent organization. A minority of libraries rely on commercial e-mail services like Yahoo! and Gmail. It will not be possible for every library to operate its own instant messaging service, for lack of staff, expertise, technology and cash.

But where individual organizations can't provide individual services, there are still alternatives to relying completely on commercial instant messaging services. Libraries can lobby their parent organizations to host enterprise IM servers, and can hopefully influence them to adopt progressive instant messaging policies. They can join together in consortial services and encourage state library agencies to offer XMPP services as state-wide programs.

Libraries don't always have the resources of internet giants like Google, or the creativity of start-ups like Meebo, but there's no reason why we can't use our own tools to build our remote reference services. When we set policies for library services, it is better to base them on our values, and not on the limitations of commercial technology available to us.

## *In summary*

Enterprise IM is nothing new. Caleb points out that organizations with a desire to control their IM communications for various reasons – records retention, privacy, network security, protection of trade secrets, enforcement of communications standards – have set up and run their own servers for IM communications for a long time. There are a number of commercial products out there to support enterprise IM, like Microsoft Live Communications Server, IBM Lotus SameTime and AOL's AIM Pro. Libraries have not, though, been big users of enterprise IM. After all, most of us started using IM precisely because it is so easy, lightweight and free. As we start to look at viable methods for

**Table 8.2** **XMPP servers and clients**

| | |
|---|---|
| **XMPP servers** | |
| | Jabberd |
| | Openfire |
| | ejabberd |
| | djabberd |
| | Jabber XCP |
| | Tigase |
| **Clients that support XMPP** | |
| | Trillian Pro |
| | Pidgin |
| | iChat |
| | Adium |
| | Meebo |
| | Psi |
| | Digsby |

using IM collaboratively, as we search for ways to make IM scale to do what we need it to, we now have a powerful motivation to run our own XMPP servers (see Table 8.2).

## Collaborative IM

As Caleb points out, there are lots of reasons we might want to set up our own IM servers – local IM networks for securely transmitting patron information between service points, barring abusive patrons, keeping statistics, utilizing 'transports' to consolidate services, eliminating viruses and worms. We think one of the most exciting developments comes in the area of collaborative IM.

IM reference has been more popular in smaller libraries. Kate Gronemyer from OSU Cascades mentions this in her piece for this book. Part of the reason for this is that smaller libraries have often lacked the resources for more fully featured virtual reference projects. Just as important, though, is the fact that IM reference scales better to the needs of a small library. The fact that only one librarian at a time can monitor the IM account is problematic for some bigger libraries. Wouldn't it be great if the message could go to a number of librarians and the first available person could answer the question? Wouldn't it be nice to be able to transfer a patron to another librarian, for instance a subject specialist? These are things that commercial IM products simply haven't been able to offer us. That's changed, though!

We're going to illustrate this new world of collaborative IM by talking about the LibraryH3lp project. It is not, we'd like to note, the only option out there, but LibraryH3lp is exciting because it is being developed by a librarian for libraries!

## *Building LibraryH3lp*

Pam Sessoms of North Carolina State University and her colleagues Josh Boyer (University of North Carolina at Chapel Hill) and Amy VanScoy (North Carolina State University) tell the story of LibraryH3lp:

> Pam Sessoms sits in her office in the Reference Department at Davis Library at the University of North Carolina at Chapel Hill (UNC). Her library's chat computers are just outside her door so she can keep an eye on all the activity. Two of UNC's reference desk staff are busily typing away at chat and IM sessions with patrons. One librarian has just transferred a patron on Yahoo! Messenger to the Circulation Department. Glancing at the logs, Pam is happy to see that Circ picked the chat up immediately and is in the process of doing its usual excellent job assisting this patron. And earlier in the week a whole bunch of UNC

students received excellent reference help late at night on IM from librarians at Duke University and North Carolina State University (NCSU) after UNC's reference desk had closed.

But the thing that tickles Pam the most is that UNC's library staff and students think all of this is perfectly normal. They don't need to know that in most of the rest of the world, two people cannot simultaneously monitor one Yahoo! Messenger account, or that it's pretty much unheard of to be able to transfer IMs from one service desk to another.

It's been a lot of work and it seems like it's taken a long time, but really things have happened awfully quickly in the end. It all began in 2003 when Duke, NCSU and UNC teamed up to extend their virtual reference services into the late-night hours. The resulting 'Night Owl' collaboration allowed the three libraries to extend service to midnight five nights a week by sharing the task of providing the service. While this collaboration sounds simple, configuring web chat software designed for a single institution to work for three was a challenge. We negotiated with the web chat software provider to create special accounts, adjusted our procedures and accepted some less than optimal configurations. But the dramatic increase in usage statistics was worth all the effort.

Around 2005, however, usage began to plateau. In addition, all three libraries had developed highly successful IM services that we were operating separately during the day. We dearly wanted Night Owl to incorporate IM, but it seemed logistically and technically impossible. We talked about it. It went something like this:

> OK, so the AIM accounts can stay connected if more than one librarian signs in. But there is that weird

> error message, and it's possible for one librarian to kick the other librarians off. Not ideal, but we can work with it. Oh, wait, if two patrons are getting help at the same time, it gets strange since messages can be going to more than one person. Hmmm, confusing, but yeah, we can deal. Next problem: Yahoo! and MSN both disconnect when a second librarian signs in. What if the staff call each other to be sure it's 'safe' to sign in, and then only pick up those accounts once they're sure? Not so bad at one institution, but it's a much bigger problem with the collaboration, where getting to all the librarians at once is nearly impossible. No way to tell if a new session started in the meantime, and if a second login occurs during a time when the first login had a chat going, that chat is disconnected. Maybe we can have all the staff on their own personal IM accounts at the same time and touch base that way... But how do we keep each other informed of individual librarian chat schedules, so that we know who is actually online for assigned public service rather than being routinely signed into their own personal account? How do we deal with having all the passwords to the various services at each campus? How do the MeeboMe accounts work for more than one simultaneous login? Oh bother, this will never work!

These headaches reminded us of the basic problem that instant messaging is built on the premise that a buddy name belongs to an individual. AIM, Yahoo! and the other IM services assume that 'davisrefdesk' is one person. They have no reason to build in features to share a buddy name across a whole reference department, much less dozens of people scattered across three libraries in three towns. We were trying to use the wrong tool for the job. However, it was the right tool for reaching our students, so we had to make it work, somehow.

When Pam's husband Eric, a programmer, caught wind of all these problems, the wheels started to turn. He decided he could do something fairly modest to at least let the Night Owl service move into the IM realm. Eric's initiative ushered in the next great phase of the Night Owl collaboration. We went live with his 'Pidgin4Lib' peer-to-peer system in fall 2007 and saw an immediate jump in usage statistics. UNC's Night Owl stats, for example, increased 300 per cent over the previous semester. NCSU found that the two-thirds of patrons were opting for the anonymous chat widget provided through Pidgin4Lib as opposed to using their personal IM accounts. In addition, numerous daily frustrations that we had accepted as a part of providing virtual reference service were improved. Shift changes and statistics gathering were easier, for example. And having Pam and Eric available to answer numerous questions from the three libraries was not bad either!

However, not everything was rosy. Pidgin4Lib was, after all, a peer-to-peer solution that relied on client software on many, many computers scattered across three towns. As bugs reared their ugly heads, we had to scurry around to a lot of different PCs to apply patches. Our librarians could not really block the occasional abusive patron since that had to get done from a 'dispatch' computer that they probably didn't have ready access to. Our librarians could not tell when patrons using the anonymous MeeboMe option had left the chat, so they wasted a lot of time replying to patrons who were no longer there. And just getting the whole thing set up initially was very confusing. It was too easy for too many staff to make small errors configuring Pidgin4Lib on lots of computers, most of them not immediately accessible to Pam and Eric. The thought of expanding Pidgin4Lib to libraries beyond our core group made Pam's hair stand on end.

Speaking of hair standing on end, Eric was not terribly excited at the prospect fixing all of this in Pidgin4Lib. Having only Pidgin, the client piece of the puzzle, to work with was just so limiting. If only he could get his hands around the server pieces too... Eric loves hard problems, and we'd proven that the basic concept was good and that our students were using the service a great deal. The decision to build LibraryH3lp, which would be able to scale and grow in ways that Pidgin4Lib simply could not, was an exciting prospect. So many pieces already existed: ejabberd, an excellent Jabber server, IM gateways and several other components were there, but they needed a lot of customization to suit our purposes, and plenty more needed to be written from scratch. Eric went to work again.

As of this writing in April 2008, we are at the cusp of another big change in our collaborative virtual reference service. We're still using Pidgin4Lib for the most part in our production services. UNC has had a LibraryH3lp widget up for a few months, but it's all feeding into Pidgin4Lib at the back end so that we can continue our collaboration. LibraryH3lp now has support for multiple librarians watching incoming queues and IM gateways for AIM, Yahoo! and MSN, and the code for transcripts and transfers is being written right now. Still to come is a Jabber-to-Jabber gateway to integrate Google Talk and perhaps other Jabber-based accounts, an improved administration web interface, a web-based librarian client for monitoring the service and a whole bunch of testing and implementation. This summer, we're looking forward to switching to LibraryH3lp entirely.

Call center chat software suits the needs of many companies and libraries. It is built for institutional use. Its fatal flaw from our point of view as librarians is that it creates a chat mechanism cut off from IM, the preferred chat method of nearly all our patrons. We are determined to build the best of both worlds – some of the administrative features of call center software that libraries need, plus the ability to chat with patrons in the IM clients they prefer.

Pam and Eric are in their living room. It's late on a Saturday afternoon and they are surrounded by a small herd of computers of various sorts. Mac OS X, Ubuntu Linux, Windows XP and Windows Vista are all accounted for, as are a few different web browsers and IM programs. Eric pushed a new release of LibraryH3lp out to the live server earlier. Things are going fine for the moment: traffic on the server appears to be normal, and numerous test chats have shown no problems. Pam likes to think of times like this as 'geeky domestic bliss'. There is some additional stress associated with being responsible for the well-being of a service used by others. If LibraryH3lp ultimately provides a platform that allows librarians to focus more on helping their patrons in the best way possible rather than working around limitations in the technology, it will have been worth it.

## How LibraryH3lp works

We hope that this description of the LibraryH3lp project got you excited, thinking about the new flexibility available to libraries offering IM reference. Pam and company developed

LibraryH3lp to support the needs of a collaborative IM reference service spread across several campuses, but the queuing and routing offered by LibraryH3lp could be helpful within a single library.

We'll explain in a little more depth how LibraryH3lp works. It's a bit more complicated than the very basic IM set-up we have discussed so far in this book. Remember, too, that LibraryH3lp is in its early stages, and the specifics we detail here might change considerably. That said, we think it is useful to explain the basics to you here so you can get a sense of how this works and how you might use it in your environment.

You need to understand the three components of LibraryH3lp: queues, gateways and operators. This gets a little complicated because it differs from the basic models we've been looking at throughout the book. Basically, each queue will forward messages from a variety of IM accounts to a number of operators, as indicated in Figure 8.7. Gateways are set up for each of the accounts you wish to monitor through a particular queue. These are called 'gateways' because the LibraryH3lp software is setting up a gateway to the various services/protocols (e.g. AIM or Yahoo!). Operators are those who answer IMs.

**Figure 8.7** Gateways, queues and operators in LibraryH3lp

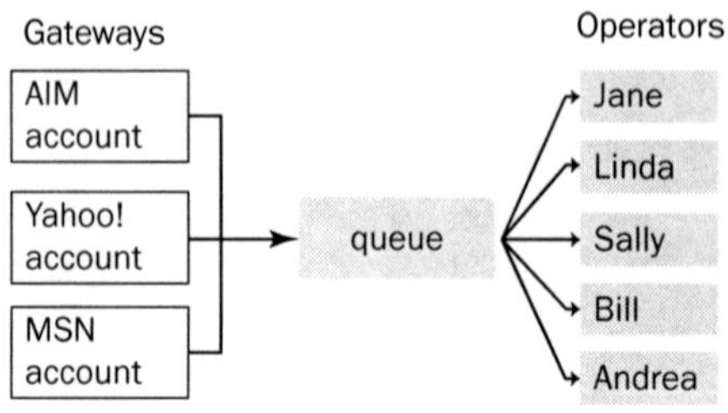

**Figure 8.8** Adding a queue

## Queues

From a central administration site, currently at libraryh3lp.com, you create one or more 'queues' (see Figure 8.8). These queues will bring together all of the accounts that you'd like to use – your AIM account, your Yahoo! account, etc. – and forward the message on to the librarians. Many, perhaps most, libraries will only need one queue. For example, if my library has three IM accounts, one on AIM, one on Yahoo! and one on MSN, all of which are currently answered at a single service point, I probably only need one queue. However, if I am part of a large library system with a set of IM accounts for each location's reference desk, I might require a queue for each of those service points or I might want one queue total.

## Gateways

Once you set up your queue, you add 'gateways' to it. The gateways are, in essence, your IM accounts. You'll create gateways for your AIM, Yahoo!, MSN and other accounts. You might, indeed, have multiple accounts with each of these that you'd like to consolidate in one queue.

So, for instance, you might have a queue called 'MainReference' that you want to route all of your accounts through. Within that queue you'd make a gateway for each of the accounts you'd like to monitor through that queue. In Figure 8.9 we have a gateway already set up for the Yahoo! account with the screen name 'libraryrachel' and we're setting one up for the AIM account 'libraryrachelb'.

Figure 8.9 Adding gateways

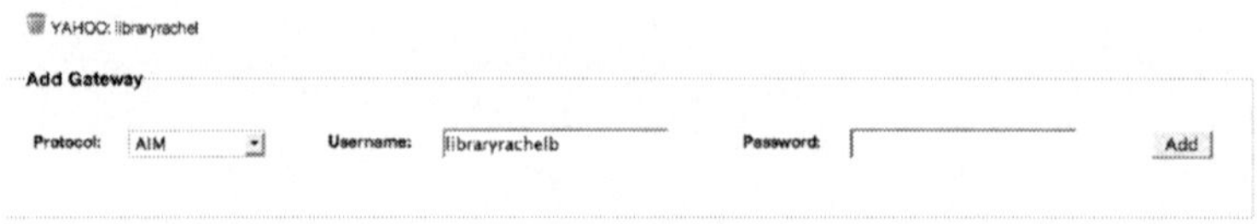


With queues and gateways you have everything in place that you need to use the LibraryH3lp widget. Simply add the LibraryH3lp Jabber account information to your client, like Pidgin or Adium, and use the widget like you would any other.

Where it gets exciting, though, is when you start adding 'operators' to your queue! When a queue has multiple operators (adding operators is shown in Figure 8.10), IMs that come into that queue will go to any operator currently signed on.

## Operators

The first operator to 'answer' the IM takes 'ownership' of that IM transaction. This allows multiple librarians to monitor a single IM account. Additionally, operators can transfer chats to one another. Those thorny scalability questions we've discussed throughout this book are solved!

LibraryH3lp is currently free to all users and free hosting is provided. Over time, a fee for hosting the IM server will likely be instituted. That said, LibraryH3lp is open source

Figure 8.10 Adding an operator

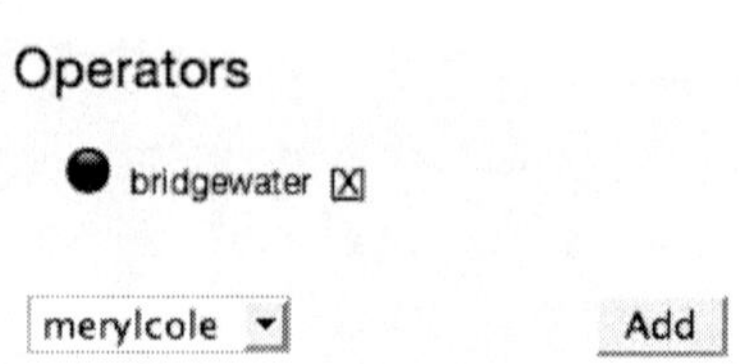

software so you can set up your own LibraryH3lp server if that makes more sense for your library. We will probably continue to see interesting developments in this area in the coming years as IM continues to mature.

## Summary

As you can see, there are a number of things you can do to make your IM reference service more sophisticated and better able to meet your patrons' needs and your staffing constraints. Widgets bring the convenience of IM reference to patrons who don't use IM or who are not currently signed into their IM clients. Widgets also offer your patrons the ability to chat anonymously.

We also explored briefly the world of enterprise instant messaging and the promise enterprise IM holds for us to take control of our own services and use IM in a way that works with our values.

Finally, we see how the technology is evolving to allow us to use IM collaboratively through LibraryH3lp or other projects and initiatives like it.

# 9

# Issues with IM reference

We love IM and think it is an incredibly easy and positive way to enhance your service offerings, but it certainly isn't without its issues. None of these issues is insurmountable, but it is worth taking some time to think about potential downsides and troubles before they become a problem for you. We see the issues facing IM reference as falling into these general categories:

- patron privacy;
- security;
- spam/spim;
- 'culture';
- workplace;
- staffing/scalability;
- cost;
- harassment.

We hope this chapter gives you the tools you'll need to address these issues for your own institution.

## Privacy

Protection of patron privacy is one of the first concerns most librarians have when the subject of IM reference comes up.

Indeed, our professional ethics require that reference questions be held in confidence – that we do all that we can to ensure our patrons' privacy. That this would be our first concern is appropriate and, unfortunately, IM reference does present some challenges to our beliefs and practices concerning patron privacy. In general, IM reference can only be as private as the service providers' privacy policies allow. These privacy policies vary, but generally do not provide the level of privacy we would prefer for our reference transactions. Additionally, IM messages are transmitted unencrypted, in plain text, and are easy for even a fairly unskilled hacker to intercept.

Many libraries have been providing e-mail reference for years and, in this regard, are used to providing reference service in conditions that are less than ideal for privacy. Perhaps our sense of urgency around the privacy issue is heightened when it comes to instant messaging because IM is relatively new to most of our organizations. Perhaps it is because the instant and immediate nature of the IM conversation tends to produce a feeling of *increased* privacy – the hallway conversation and water-cooler gossip of the world of electronic communication. Whatever the reason, we are correct to be sensitized to the privacy issues surrounding IM.

When we consider privacy in the context of IM reference we're really talking about two different sets of privacy practices: the privacy policies of third-party service providers, and local privacy policies and practices.

## *Privacy policies of third-party service providers*

Service providers such as AOL and Yahoo! make their instant messaging services available to the public free of charge. Part of what these companies get in return for this service is eyeballs for advertising. Another thing they get is access to a fair amount of information about how their customers use their services. The user agrees to the privacy policy developed by the service provider and, in exchange, can use the IM network and services of that provider. It is important to remember that, regardless of what kind of policies you put in place locally, your interactions on IM will be governed by the privacy policies of the providers you and your patron are using. As of this writing, most of the major IM providers (AOL, Yahoo! and MSN) had similar provisions in their privacy policies. All provide aggregate information to advertisers and 'partners'; all collect information about access and use patterns; all will turn over the contents of IM conversations (or other private information) in response to court orders or subpoenas. All also indicate that records will be shared and conversations read when unlawful or dangerous activity is suspected. In other words, none of the major providers actually requires a court order in order to share records with law enforcement or anyone else. We don't point this out to cause alarm, but to make our readers aware that the privacy policies of service providers are considerably out of sync with the privacy standards of most libraries.

## *Local privacy practices*

Though you cannot directly control the privacy practices of the IM service providers, you can control the privacy protection measures you put into place at your library. There are simple steps, like thoughtful management of *logs* and *contact lists*, you can take to ensure that your local practices do not unnecessarily compromise patron privacy. Your organization might decide to explore more advanced methods of protecting privacy, like the use of *widgets* or *encryption*. In the pages that follow, we'll explore these local practices.

## Logs

Your IM software will give you the option of creating logs for all of your IM conversations. IM logs are complete transcripts of your chats. Instant messaging software is not designed to handle logs in a manner that protects patron privacy. When logging is enabled, logs are stored in plain text in a designated folder on your computer and remain there unless deleted. These logs can be terrific tools for assessment, training and patron follow-up. However, they can also raise privacy questions.

Some things to think about while you're deciding how to handle your IM logs are access; retention schedule; logging by IM management software; public records; and morale.

- *Access.* If you should decide to keep logs of IM conversations for training or assessment purposes, you will need to make some decisions about how to handle those logs. First, who has access to them? If logs are being stored on a shared reference computer on a public floor, everyone who has access to that computer will have access to the logs. This might be desirable if you want all the librarians to read one another's transcripts for training purposes. If this isn't desirable and you do want to maintain logs, you will need to come up with a procedure for transferring the logs to a different location. Most IM software does not allow for any sophisticated handling of logs, so it will be a largely manual process should you decide to do this. In other words, you could have a librarian routinely e-mail the log to a supervisor or place the log file on a more secure drive after completing a chat. This does, however, add significant workload to the librarian conducting the chat.

- *Retention schedule*. Developing a retention schedule for your logs is essential if you decide to enable logging. You will be amazed at how quickly the logs pile up for even a lightly used IM service! Each of these logs is a complete record of an interaction with a patron. They should be treated very much in the same way as we treat other patron records: respectfully, carefully and with solid policies backing us up. Decide how long your logs will be kept and try to make this retention period appropriate to your intended use. If you are retaining logs with the goal of service assessment, for example, will you review those logs daily? Weekly? Quarterly? Can they be deleted after they have been reviewed? Can information from the logs be anonymized for analysis purposes? Decide how long you need to keep these logs and delete them when you don't need them any more.
- *Automatic logging by IM management software*. On the subject of logging, it is probably useful to mention that many organizations have invested in IM management software such as Symantec IM Manager to help them manage the impact of IM on their businesses. This software is designed to allow businesses to control instant messaging on their internal networks by sending all the IM traffic through a central server at the business. These tools offer protection from security threats like viruses and other malware. They also allow companies to filter outgoing messages for content to prevent loss of intellectual property, for instance. Finally, the software allows a business to have sense of how much its employees are using IM for personal matters. Be aware that if you are operating in an institution with IM

management software in place, you will need to factor that into your decision about the provision of IM reference. In such a scenario, logs would automatically be created and stored on the server and would likely be out of the direct control of library personnel.

- *Public records.* Some companies and organizations use IM management software to ensure that they comply with regulations regarding record retention. This is something you'll need to consider too, depending on the kind of organization you're working in. If your library requires that you retain e-mails and other communications, it is possible (even likely) that IM records should be retained as well.
- *Morale.* Finally, it is important to consider how retention of logs will affect the morale of the library staff conducting IM reference. We discussed this at greater length in Chapter 5 but will quickly review the issues here. Reference staff may feel that they are being unfairly monitored if their chat logs are retained, especially if a supervisor is reviewing those logs to assess and evaluate the quality of reference service. We can always look back at an individual interaction with a patron and wish that we had done or said something differently. Avoid the temptation to go over the logged chats with a fine-toothed comb. Be clear with your staff about how you will be using the chat logs and what kind of feedback they can expect from you regarding those chats.

## Contact list

Another easily implemented local privacy practice is the careful management of the contact list. By default, your IM software might add people who send you messages to your contact list. If you are interested in maximizing patron privacy, you will want to change this setting. As a matter of course, leaving patrons off your contact list is the best policy. Having them on your contact list is an indication that the library has communicated with them; there is no sense in retaining that information. In general, IM service will be initiated by the patron, so adding patrons to your contact list will offer little or no benefit to your service. You may have local exceptions to this general practice – for instance, if you provide regular research support for known patrons, e.g. in a special library or to faculty, you may wish to add them to your contact list.

## Encryption

Many IM programs offer optional encryption features or extensions/plug-ins. Put simply, encryption makes the data being transferred back and forth on the internet by the two parties participating in an IM session more difficult for third parties to read. As discussed earlier, IM messages are, by default, transmitted in plain text, allowing them to be easily intercepted and read by third parties. Encryption encodes the messages sent over the IM network, making them more difficult to 'crack'.

There are several different kinds of encryption.

- *Secure Socket Layer (SSL).* Most internet users are familiar with SSL: it is the same kind of encryption used by most websites to protect credit card information or other private personal data. SSL requires no configuration or set-up on the part of the IM user, it 'just works'. Use of SSL requires that the IM network you're using supports it. For instance, Google Talk (which uses the XMPP protocol) provides SSL support both natively and in the clients that support it (like Adium and Pidgin).

- *Off-the-Record (OTR).* OTR is an increasingly popular and well-supported form of encryption. OTR uses keys for authentication but, as implemented, does so fairly unobtrusively. In addition to encryption and authentication, OTR offers 'deniability' and 'perfect forward secrecy'. Sounds pretty cloak-and-dagger, doesn't it? Deniability means that the digital signatures which assure your correspondent that you are who you say you are aren't checkable by a third party. So anyone could, conceivably, forge a message after a conversation to make it look like it came from you. Why is this a good thing? Because no one can prove you said anything! It could always have been an imposter! 'Perfect forward secrecy' means that if you lose control of your private keys, no previous conversation has been compromised. Does all of this sound really confusing to you? Don't worry. All you *really* need to understand about OTR is that it provides a way for your conversations to be private provided that both parties are using it.
- *Simp.* Simp is a commercial product made by Secway. Simp, like OTR, encrypts your messages. Again like OTR, the person who is chatting with you must also be using Simp in order for your exchange to be encrypted. Simp works with all of the major IM services. The free version, Simp Lite, will only secure one service per computer, though, making it a poor choice for your IM reference service unless you intend to offer the service via only one provider. Simp Pro, the enterprise-level product, will allow your library to secure all the IM services you use. At the time of this writing it was priced at €4.95/$4.95 per license. Secway also offers Simp Server for Unix servers.
- *Pretty Good Privacy (PGP).* PGP is a standard encryption scheme defined by the OpenPGP standard: it is often used

for e-mail but is not a common encryption tool for IM. PGP requires the user to create and use a special key to decrypt messages meant for them. Without the key, the message can't be read. Before using PGP to exchange messages with another user the two users must exchange key information with one another. Because PGP involves such a high degree of maintenance and configuration by the user, it is not terribly practical. A handful of IM clients do support PGP, using the XMPP protocol, including Hush Messenger and Miranda. None of the major clients that we discuss in this book supports PGP.

- *SecureIM.* This is the encryption tool built into the Trillian client. SecureIM does not provide authentication.
- *Pidgin-encryption.* This is an available plug-in for the Pidgin client. It does not provide deniability or perfect forward secrecy like OTR.

So why *wouldn't* you use encryption? There are a few things to keep in mind about encrypting your IM communications with patrons. First, it only works if both parties are using it. You can certainly set your IM client up to allow encrypted chats with your patrons, but unless they are also using encryption the conversation will not be private. Second, OTR offers impressive encryption with very little user intervention but it does sometimes have unexpected results. When the client is expecting an encrypted message but doesn't get one, it can often fail or send what looks like a bunch of random characters. This is more of a nuisance than anything else but can be very disorienting when it happens.

### Anonymous chat through widgets

An increasingly popular way to provide reference service is through the use of website widgets. Because patrons are anonymous when they use your widget, this provides quite complete privacy as long as neither the librarian nor the patron shares private or personally identifying information in the course of the conversation.

## Some thoughts about privacy

The recent explosion of so-called Web 2.0 technologies and services has raised a lot of questions for librarians, not least in the area of privacy. We see that users are willing, even eager, to trade privacy for convenience and customization. In the past it was relatively easy for libraries to set policies which were protective of patrons' privacy without a serious loss of convenience or access for patrons. The current state of affairs puts us in an awkward position. Should we adopt policies and positions that protect our patrons' privacy even when they explicitly request that we do not? Where does our responsibility end? Can we justify starting a service like IM reference that we know to be dubious with regard to privacy even if we put all possible safeguards in place?

We would argue that, yes, we can certainly justify such services. Indeed, perhaps we can use our interactions with our patrons over IM as a way of engaging them in a conversation about privacy. If a patron begins to offer personal information such as ID numbers during an IM conversation, try stopping them and say something like 'I'm happy to take your student ID number over IM but I thought I would point out that IM, like e-mail, isn't a secure way to share information. Perhaps you'd like to give us a call?' With this quick interaction, you've done a couple of things: given patrons control over their own privacy decisions, and perhaps informed them about the privacy risks inherent in IM and e-mail. In our interactions with patrons we've had such exchanges on many occasions. The most frequent response is a stunned 'E-mail isn't secure?!?!' IM reference may, indeed, provide the perfect model for library privacy practices: the library does everything possible to secure the interaction at its end, the side the library controls, and gives users 'permission' to control the level of privacy they set at their own end. In such a model, we assert that the library has a role in educating patrons in a proactive way about the privacy and security options available to them. If we see internet security and privacy practices as part of what it takes to be an effective citizen in the post-internet world, we can see that this kind of work fits perfectly with the missions of most libraries.

## Security

Security concerns are always high on the list of questions people raise when considering starting an IM reference service. We have heard many anecdotes of IM being banned by IT departments based on security concerns. It is our opinion that the security issues involved with IM can be managed with a minimum of care. Kim and Leem (2005) outline the risks associated with IM and identify measures that we can take to mitigate those risks. As their paper is fairly comprehensive in terms of raising all possible risks, we will use the risks Kim and Leem have enumerated as a framework for this section. We'll look at each of these risks, examine their importance in a library setting and discuss some possible solutions.

Kim and Leem (ibid.) raise the following IM security issues:

- viruses/worms/trojans;
- eavesdropping on unencrypted communications;

- information loss;
- spam;
- impersonation;
- identity theft;
- tracking;
- theft of message logging;
- copyright violation.

## *Risk: viruses/worms/trojans*

Users can transfer files to one another without going through any centralized IT filtering (as is often done with e-mail). If users open an infected file, the virus can spread to the user's machine and maybe your whole network.

This risk is similar to the risk we face with e-mail, but because e-mail passes through a central server at your organization there is some opportunity to check for viruses before the e-mail is delivered to the user.

Relevance for libraries: high.

### Potential solutions

- *Technical.* Make sure all virus scanning software is up to date. Store received files only on a computer with a virus scanner installed.
- *Training/education.* Train all employees using IM about the risks associated with accepting files.
- *Policy.* Create strict policies about how employees should use IM. For instance, in most libraries a policy against accepting *any* file via IM would be reasonable.

## *Risk: eavesdropping on unencrypted communications*

The security/privacy concerns related to the clear-text transmission of IM messages was discussed at length in the 'privacy' section of this chapter. In short, IM messages are transmitted over the internet in clear text. Though IM conversations may feel quite private and secure to users of the software, messages are actually quite easily intercepted by third parties.

Relevance for libraries: high.

### Potential solutions

- *Technical.* Encryption software is available for many IM programs. Remember that both parties must be using encryption software, so this will rarely be a full solution in patron service situations. For more about encryption software, read the privacy section of this chapter.
- *Training/education.* As discussed in the previous section, librarians should be trained to understand the risks associated with transferring private data over IM. They should certainly not ask patrons to divulge private information via IM – at least not without having a full conversation with the patron about the risks involved. Reference interactions on IM also provide a terrific opportunity for the librarian to educate the patron about the security/privacy implications of using IM.

## *Risk: information loss*

Many enterprise IT departments put strict file size limitations on e-mail messages in order to discourage the easy sharing of secret/valuable documents. Because IM software is generally outside the control of enterprise IT departments, these file size limitations aren't enforceable on IM.

Relevance for libraries: varied. This risk is relevant mostly to businesses with trade secrets and other valuable information to protect. In most library environments this will probably not be a serious issue. Corporate librarians are likely to face concerns from their IT department about this.

### Potential solutions

- *Technical.* Company IT departments can implement monitoring software that will detect outgoing files and/or check for keywords etc.
- *Policy.* Create strict policies about how employees should use IM. For instance, create a policy prohibiting employees from sending certain kinds of information out using IM.

## *Risk: spam*

Instant messaging spam, or 'spim', will be discussed at length later in this chapter. From our perspective this falls into the category of 'annoyance' more than it does 'security concern'.

## *Risk: impersonation*

It is very easy to register a screen name on most IM services. The screen name does not have to be related in any way to a user's actual name. As a result, it would be fairly trivial for someone to create an IM user name intended to fool potential correspondents into believing they are someone they are not. For instance, as long as the screen name wasn't taken, someone could register a screen name that seemed to be Rachel – something like RachelBridgewaterReed – and then impersonate Rachel in order to obtain information or tarnish her reputation.

Relevance for libraries: moderate. As our patrons are largely anonymous or semi-anonymous when they message us, we are unlikely to fall victim to impersonators at that end. We should be concerned, however, about the possibility of a malicious user attempting to impersonate us – in other words a disgruntled, mischievous or otherwise unethical patron registering a screen name like YourLibrarysName.

### Potential solutions

- *Training/education.* Broadly publicize your screen name so that users become familiar with your valid screen name.
- *Policy.* Create standard formats for screen names within your institution. You might consider creating multiple screen names so that all convenient variations on your library's name will already be taken if you believe this is a serious risk among your user population.

## *Risk: identity theft*

Kim and Leem (ibid.) assert that 'IM is more prone than email to damage caused by identity theft. Getting access to another's IM identity can be as simple as sitting down at a deserted desktop.' We remain unconvinced that IM really presents a greater risk than e-mail, but the risk does exist. If you choose to run IM from your reference desk, be aware that anyone could walk up and pretend to be you if the desk is left unmonitored. Likewise, if patrons regularly use IM from computers within your library, they do risk having their IM session appropriated if they walk away from the computer without logging out.

Relevance for libraries: low to moderate. We've discussed the major issues involved with the clear-text transmission of data in IM in other sections of the chapter. We see this as the biggest risk for identity theft when using these services.

### Potential solutions

- *Technical.* Lock your desktop (via screensaver or other method) when not at your computer. Install management software on your computers that will require login/logout by patrons.
- *Training/education.* Pick hard-to-crack passwords. Teach patrons to log off their IM sessions when leaving a public computer.

## *Risk: tracking*

One key component of IM services is presence awareness. In other words, the software is designed to transmit information regarding users' status: signed in, signed out, idle, away, etc. This kind of information is essential for the operation of IM; you need to know if your 'buddy' is available if you want to send them a message.

Relevance for libraries: low. Kim and Leem (ibid.) frame this presence tracking issue in terms of corporate competitiveness. They indicate that competitors could use this feature of IM to determine when top executives are working late and the like. This is rarely going to be an issue in a library setting. However, there are potential personal safety issues involved with this that might be relevant to libraries. It is those issues we'll address in our solutions.

### Potential solutions

- *Technical.* Allow only buddies to track presence.
- *Policy.* Do not set detailed away messages, indicating where you will be and when, if personal safety issues are pressing in your environment.

## *Risk: theft of message logging*

If you have opted to log your messages (more on this in the privacy section of this chapter), these logs are stored as simple text files. These files are easy to copy – small, unencrypted and easily located. Any personal information stored within those logs would then be available to the thief.

Relevance for libraries: low to moderate.

### Potential solutions

- *Technical.* The simplest solution is just to turn logging off. You could also store your files in an encrypted format using encryption software.
- *Policy.* Make it your policy not to log IM conversations. If IM conversations are logged, have a retention/management policy in place so that those logs are deleted regularly.

## *Risk: copyright violation*

The risk of copyright and database license violation is yet another risk associated with IM because of the file transfer features available in this software. While chatting with a patron in need of an article in a database, it might be most expedient simply to send the patron that file. However, recall that database licenses and copyright provisions limit the uses we may make of many of our resources.

Relevance for libraries: high.

### Potential solutions

- *Training/education.* Make sure all reference staff have sufficient understanding of the laws and licenses governing the use of copyrighted library materials to assess accurately the copyright/license situations presented to them.
- *Policy.* Various policy solutions are available to prevent the inappropriate transmittal of copyrighted materials. A policy restricting all file transfers would be the most extreme. Your library could also set a policy that the patron's affiliation with the library must be confirmed before library resources are delivered to that patron electronically.

## *Corporate IT policy*

Like all internet communications, IM does have security issues associated with it. But with a careful combination of policies, training and technical measures the risk associated with IM should be very low. However, corporate librarians face a different set of issues. Jason Eiseman, a law librarian, fleshes a few out for us.

> Every library has its own IT policy. Some libraries may have their own IT departments, and the ability to set the policy at a library level. For those libraries, implementing instant messaging reference services may be as simple as convincing library administration of its value. For other libraries implementing IM reference may be as easy as signing up for an online service.

However, corporate libraries are often at the mercy of the corporation IT department policy, which can limit how libraries in those organizations can implement an IM reference service, and administrations which have more on their mind than efficient library services.

Even while the use of IM in corporations has risen, security concerns have also continued to rise. IM programs which require downloads, software installation or browser plug-ins are often discouraged or even banned in corporations. Concerns over data security, viruses and conflicts with business-critical software have led some corporate IT departments to implement a near-lockdown status on employee computers. Some corporations have also blocked IM to prevent the drain on network resources.

In addition to the security concerns of IT, there are also concerns about the potential liability caused by employee use of IM. There are concerns about the liability caused by harassment, and damage to productivity. But there are also specific legal concerns as well. The potential for employees to leak proprietary information about valuable intellectual property has scared off some organizations. Recent legal developments in electronic discovery have also raised the issue of how to archive IM conversations for legal compliance.

Despite these concerns many corporations have implemented IM as part of their internal communications systems. There are also software vendors which have developed enterprise IM services as part of their services. These solutions have addressed at least some of the concerns about IM in corporations, and provide opportunities for corporate libraries to implement IM services.

Corporate libraries should work with their IT departments to implement IM reference services. Corporate employees may use specialized enterprise IM software to connect users, without exposing secured data on external servers. Connecting with corporate users on the platforms they use is essential to implementing an IM reference service.

It is also important that the library use of IM reference services fits into the corporate culture. Although there may be an IM solution available for library services, librarians must ensure that the employees will buy into reference transactions conducted over IM.

There is a future for IM reference service in corporate libraries. However, it is often difficult to navigate the obstacles that can impede the implementation of IM services. Working with the corporate IT department, human resource and other administration officials is essential to navigating the complex technical, legal and administrative atmosphere in the corporate environment. (Jason Eiseman, Schwabe, Williamson & Wyatt)

## Spam/spim

We are all familiar with the pervasive problem of e-mail 'spam' messages: the unsolicited commercial e-mail, often generated or spread by computer programs or 'bots', which clogs our inboxes every day. Unfortunately, spam can be a problem for users of instant messaging software as well. IM spam is often referred to as spim.

The bad news is that one of the most effective ways of countering spim is, sadly, not practical for the library reference service. Many users choose to accept messages only from people already on their contact lists. This is a very effective way of weeding out spim for the average user. Your reference desk account, though, will likely accept messages *primarily* from people not on its contact list. As we discussed in the privacy section of this chapter, you should avoid adding patrons to your contact list.

The good news is that most IM networks have become quite good at combating spim. In the two years that we have been providing IM reference service, we've never received a spim message. Nowadays, spim seems to be under control to the point where it is a minor annoyance at worst. However, it is definitely something to keep an eye on!

## Culture issues

People communicate differently depending on the channel for that communication. We know this is true – that a letter is different from a phone call is different from an e-mail is different from a memo is different from face-to-face communication – but the 'culture' of IM unnerves some librarians nonetheless.

### *Casual*

IM communication is exceedingly casual. Those who bemoan the formality and care for the written word that were lost in the move to e-mail will find the world of IM troubling in the extreme. Proper grammar, spelling and punctuation are considered unnecessary time-wasters in the vernacular of IM. IM conversations have more in common with face-to-face communication than formal written communications, even e-mail. One obvious manifestation of the casual ‘speed before accuracy’ nature of IM is the abbreviated language often used in IM conversations. We’ve provided a list of some common abbreviations in Table 9.1. This list isn’t exhaustive, but we feel that most of the abbreviations you’re likely to encounter will be included.

**Table 9.1** **IM language – a brief primer**

| | |
|---|---|
| b4n, bfn | bye for now |
| bbl | be back later |
| brb | be right back |
| c | see |
| convo | conversation |
| fwiw | for what it’s worth |
| <g> | user is grinning/smiling |
| idk | I don’t know |
| jk | just kidding |
| l8r | later |
| lmao | laughing my ass off |
| lol | laugh/laughing out loud |
| np | no problem |
| omg | oh my gosh/God |
| otoh | on the other hand |
| ppl | people |
| r | are |
| rotfl | rolling on the floor laughing |
| thx | thanks |
| ttyl | talk to you later |
| u | you |
| w00t! | expression of joy/enthusiasm |
| wrt | with regard/respect to |
| y | why? |
| ymmv | your mileage may vary (your experience might be different) |

### *Pace*

Paradoxically, although individual responses in an IM conversation are generally pithy and speedy, the overall conversation may take place over a very long period of time. IM users are typically multitasking on their computers and recognize that the presence indicators provided by IM software represent a sort of general availability but don't imply that the user on the other end will be able to talk with them immediately. In other words, your users will probably expect that you have a bunch of things going on and won't mind if it takes you a while to conduct your conversation. This issue of pacing is very uncomfortable for many librarians at first. We are used to providing either immediate service (in face-to-face or telephone reference) or completely asynchronous service (as with e-mail reference). IM reference represents a kind of middle ground between these two modes of service. The conversation is immediate and synchronous but may unfold over a very long period of time with delays on both sides of the conversation.

## Workplace issues

If your library decides to launch an IM reference service, you'll probably want to encourage library staff to use IM on their office computers as well. Using IM for inter-office communication will help your staff become familiar and comfortable with the IM conversational style. Right now, there is little consensus on whether IM increases or decreases worker productivity. Karen Diller, currently interim assistant vice chancellor of academic affairs at Washington State University Vancouver, discusses some of the changes in workplace communication that came about on her campus as a result of starting IM reference:

> We implemented IM reference service in our library about the same time that we hired several younger librarians. The change in our reference service was barely perceptible – we already provided e-mail, phone and in-person reference – so this was just an addition of another method. However, the surprise came when I started to realize that office communications changed dramatically. I tended to manage and communicate by walking around and planting myself in people's offices. In fact, many of us designed our offices to have at least one comfortable chair for colleagues and visitors. After IM reference was implemented, I worried because I was not seeing enough 'wandering around' by the newer, younger librarians. I was fearful that we were no longer communicating as much as we should be. However, I quickly learned that folks were communicating – and maybe even more than before – but their communication was happening online via instant messaging rather than in person via wandering about. Those of us who adapted quickly to the idea of communicating with patrons via this new method now found ourselves contemplating whether we could also adapt our office communication style to IM. For me, the jury is still out. I suspect that those who think to communicate first via technology will need to add a little exercise into their routines and those of us who think to communicate first via our feet will need to add a little more technology into ours. (Karen Diller, Washington State University Vancouver Library)

## Staffing/scalability

### *Staffing*

The question of how to staff an IM reference service effectively is one of the most pressing issues facing libraries using or thinking about using IM. Who will staff the service? When? Where? Will they be able to do other things while they staff the service or will they be so busy that it will be, essentially, like adding another desk? The answer to these questions will vary depending on your library, naturally. See Chapter 4 for a discussion of the various staffing options.

## Scalability

The staffing quandary that IM presents is largely due to the fact that by using IM in this way we are in a sense using it for a purpose for which it really wasn't designed.

To review: at its most basic, IM is designed to handle direct interactions from one person to another using a single service. Meryl and Rachel want to talk to each other? Each creates an account on the same service, they share user names, and we're off to the races (Figure 9.1).

IM clients like Pidgin, Trillian, Meebo and the like helped the situation by allowing the user to sign into all of the supported networks simultaneously (Figure 9.2).

Terrific for individual IM users! Imagine, though, Librarian A is out at the reference desk and gets an urgent IM from a chemistry professor with a complicated discipline-specific question. Librarian A, the history liaison, wants to connect the patron with Librarian B, the chemistry liaison. If the patron was on the phone, Librarian A would transfer the call. If it was an e-mail, Librarian A would

**Figure 9.1** Two Yahoo! users can chat with one another

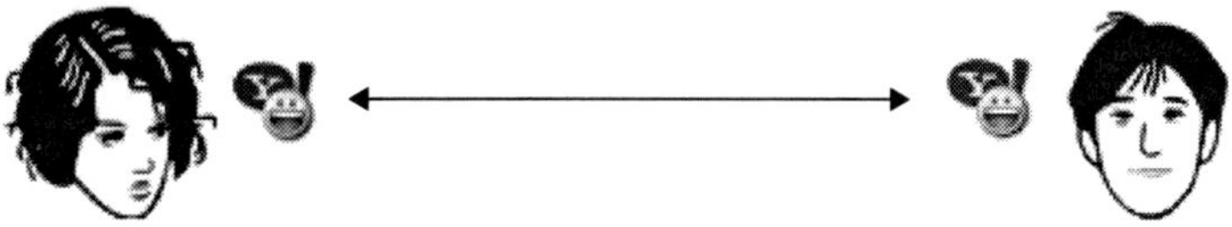

**Figure 9.2** Multi-protocol clients allow a user to sign into all her accounts at once

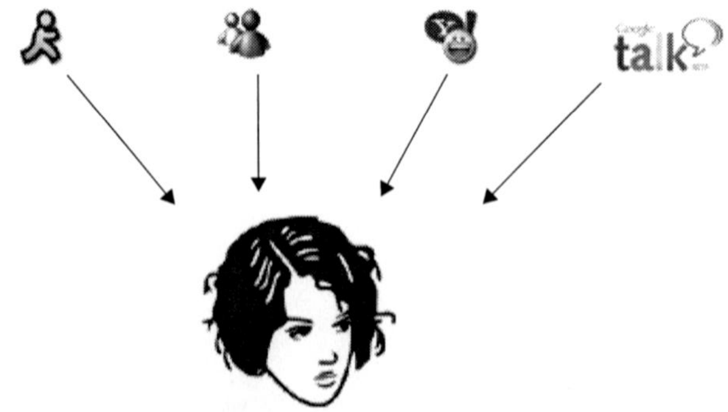


forward it. If the patron was standing in front of us, Librarian A would see if Librarian B was available to come out and chat. Unfortunately, with basic IM there is no easy way for Librarian A to transfer the patron to Librarian B.

To take another situation, Librarian C is staffing the normally rather sleepy reference desk, helping a face-to-face patron with some research. Librarian C is providing great reference service: going out to the stacks with the patron, bringing materials from the reference collection over to where the patron is working, searching along with the patron on the patron's computer. Meanwhile, back at the desk, three patrons have submitted IM reference questions and have received no response. There's no easy way for Librarian C's co-workers to know what is happening and answer the IM questions in Librarian C's absence.

Because IM is designed to facilitate conversations between individuals, it does not readily adapt to the kind of collaborative, flexible uses we want to put it to. In Chapter 8 we talked about some of the promising ways in which this is changing, highlighting tools that are available to facilitate collaborative IM. 'Out of the box', though, IM presents very real, often insurmountable, scalability issues. If your library is one for which these scalability issues are a serious problem, please do check out some of the options presented in Chapter 8.

## Costs

Instant messaging reference is a very low-cost virtual reference solution. Typically, the software itself is free. Even if you decide to use one of the very few IM clients that require payment, the fees are very low – in the range of $25/license. Some advanced solutions like enterprise IM or hosting your own IM server would have higher costs associated with them.

Staffing, though, is another matter and would be the area in which you'd be likely to see budget implications. If your IM service becomes so popular that it is necessary to add additional staff hours in order to serve the patrons clamoring at your virtual door, the costs obviously rise.

## Harassment

When we talk to librarians about reference using IM they frequently express concern that they will be harassed or, at the very least, be the target of unwanted advances and/or rudeness on IM. It is certainly true that people can and do behave differently in the anonymous or semi-anonymous world of chat than they would if they were standing at your desk. Since we all know that even while they're standing at our desks patrons can be rude or inappropriate from time to time, we're understandably concerned that we'll be forced to endure worse behavior on chat.

We suggest that you develop a policy of dealing with rude or inappropriate patrons via IM that is similar to the approach you might take in person. It is likely that your library has either stated or implied procedures for dealing with inappropriate patrons that probably include some or all of the following steps: asking the patron to refrain from the behavior, insisting that the patron refrain from the behavior, warning the patron that the transaction cannot continue if they do not refrain from the behavior and terminating the interaction. In the case of IM, it is easy to take this final step; you just have to close the window. IM offers a further step – the ability to 'block' a patron. This will prevent that user from contacting you or seeing your status online. Of course, this is unlikely to stop a truly determined harasser, who can always create a new screen name. And note that if a user engages in truly harassing behavior – that is, behavior which might be illegal, not merely irritating – you should involve the appropriate authorities, just as you would if the patron were harassing you in person.

> When we started using IM to provide reference at WSU Vancouver, none of us really knew what to expect and we'd had several conversations about what to do if a patron acted inappropriately or was rude with us. One night I was working at the reference desk and multitasking between in-person, IM and telephone reference as usual. I got an IM from a patron looking for some information; we chatted for a while and then the patron abruptly asked: 'R U the girl with the short hair?'
>
> I was immediately put on edge! Something about being asked about my appearance, combined with being referred to as a 'girl', made me really nervous. Was my patron going to try to hit on me? Why was this patron asking me this!? It did describe me, though.

I had recently gotten a very short haircut. With my heart in my throat, I answered: 'Yes, I am the librarian with short hair.'

The patron replied: 'Oh cool. i'm right over here – i'll come over.'

A young woman jumped up from one of the terminals near the reference desk and walked over to the desk, saying 'It seemed like it was getting complicated and it would be easier to do this in person.'

This was a good lesson to me about jumping to the wrong conclusion about my patron's intentions! (Rachel Bridgewater)

## Summary

As you can see, the issues associated with IM are real but manageable. Remember, too, that the risks and issues associated with any technology are not static. Take it upon yourself to see what new developments in the world of IM may have occurred since the publication of this book – these things are always a moving target!

10

# Promoting your IM reference service

Libraries, like businesses, need to market their services. Stereotypically, librarians have an aversion to marketing – perhaps because they feel libraries are such well-known institutions that no marketing is needed, or because marketing is somewhat off-putting and smarmy. In many ways this is just semantics; we encourage you to think of marketing as promotion. When you are marketing, you are simply educating your patrons about library services and reaching out to new patrons. To generate interest in and traffic to your new IM reference service, it is probably not enough to place a link or even a widget on your library's front webpage. You are creating an IM reference service to augment your offerings to your patrons and you'll want to let them know about it!

## Promote it

We know that any successful initiative begins with a plan. It is easy to put a widget on your library's main webpage or to post signs around the library advertising your IM reference service. And these are fine options. Yet they are more powerful when part of a plan than a piecemeal marketing attempt – not to mention that they reach only those who visit your website or your library. So, how do we develop a promotional campaign? For our purposes we will assume that you will mount your campaign in-house with limited financial resources. Fear not! There are many librarian-created shared marketing resources. Check the 'Marketing' section of the *Library Success: A Best Practices Wiki* for starters (www.libsuccess.org/index.php?title=Marketing). All promotional options are extensible, and if you are fortunate enough to have more resources at your disposal, go ahead and extend, expand and maybe even hire a professional!

At the outset of your planning effort consider the structure of your IM reference service. Are you one of many libraries on a college campus? Are you part of a consortium of libraries providing IM reference together? Or are you a single special library? The point is that you should consider your partner libraries and ideally build a plan together that all libraries in your group can use. KnowItNow 24x7, Ohio's successful and widely used state-wide virtual reference service, did just that. According to Tracy Strobel (2005) of the Cleveland Public Library, 'our marketing mission was to provide the local libraries with the tools they needed to promote the service in their own communities. The centerpiece of this approach was the Media Kit.' The media kit has tools that Ohio libraries can tailor to their communities and then deploy; check it out at www.knowitnow.org/mediakit.

## Target your audience

Who are you trying to reach? Determining your audience is an essential first step because it shapes the rest of your campaign. The best ideas could fall flat if marketed to the wrong audience. Don't assume that everyone who views your promotional materials will be struck by the same message and try your IM reference service in the near future.

Consider the disparate groups that make up your patron base. If you work in an academic library, perhaps it's faculty, undergraduate students and distance students. If you're in a public library, maybe you feel teenage girls are using your IM service, but you'd like to reach teenage boys. If you work in a special library, perhaps there is a particular department that you feel could benefit from your IM reference service. Keep in mind, too, that not all of your target audience will be online as much as younger patrons are, so be sure to promote the service to them differently.

Wyoming Libraries won the 2007 John Cotton Dana Award for their state-wide marketing campaign. Their goal was to increase awareness of the libraries and their services. To determine the target audience for their campaign more accurately, the University of Wyoming Survey and Analysis Center conducted a survey – for which the library sent out postcards to library card holders who had not used their cards in two years – soliciting equal numbers of men and women, and directing them to an online survey. Of the respondents, 81 per cent were women. This result, coupled with the fact that men 'make up a large portion of the decision makers in the state', led them to conclude that men should be their target audience (Lackey, 2008). It is important to note that they were mindful that though men were the target audience for the campaign, they built the campaign so that it would not offend women. Their campaign was a success! As of 2007, Wyoming has seen a 21 per cent increase in library card holders. Tina Lackey, publications and marketing manager, shares the meanings behind the campaign's logo and slogan and what makes them uniquely Wyoming.

> The new Wyoming libraries logo is a cowboy on a bucking book, reminiscent of the bucking horse and rider which is the official trademark of the State of

**Figure 10.1** Wyoming State Library promotional campaign

Courtesy of Wyoming State Library

Wyoming. Although the logo is similar to the bucking horse and rider, it is unique to libraries, due to the cowboy riding a book rather than a horse, and it is uniquely Wyoming.

The advertising agency also created a campaign around the slogan 'Bringing the World to Wyoming' [Figure 10.1]. In their designs, they showed elements of something from another part of the world that you would learn about at the library, and put it in a Wyoming setting. (Tina Lackey, Wyoming State Library)

## *Craft your message*

Now that you have your audience in mind, it is time to craft your message. In general, we know that the message will be along the lines of 'Look, we now have IM reference, come and try it!' Personalizing your message to your target audience will be more effective. Consider how IM reference could best serve them. For distance students, for example, your promotional materials could highlight the fact that they can still ask the reference librarian questions even though they live hundreds of miles away. Public libraries could promote their genealogy tools for interested patrons. If you work in a law library, perhaps some attorneys are on a conference call and need some quick information. They could IM you while continuing their call and present the information you send back seamlessly!

## Generate ideas

You've got an audience and a message, now how do you get it out? There are many options, ranging from the basic insert bookmarks advertising your IM reference service to press releases to the media and service launch parties. Brainstorm as many ideas as you can! Then determine which have the most potential and which are feasible. Be selective: do not feel that you must try every idea at once to saturate the market, as that can often work against a promotional campaign. Instead, choose the handful of options that work well and work well together, and try those first.

The aforementioned 'Marketing' section of the *Library Success: A Best Practices Wiki* lists success stories ranging from YouTube book trailers to the St Charles Library Cart Capades Bookettes, a group of librarians doing synchronized book-cart pushing. Have fun and be creative! Fun helps get the message out, and also helps remind patrons that we are indeed a fun group!

## Implement

Promote, promote, promote! Let patrons know about your IM reference service. Tell them once, twice, three times. Deploy those strategies you've decided upon.

Be enthusiastic! Take every opportunity to talk it up. Not only at the reference desk, but at the circulation desk, at instruction sessions, during meetings and lectures. Anywhere and everywhere. At the bus stop...

### *Evaluate*

Here we could agree that the measure of success is increased traffic. It is up to your library to determine how much of an increase indicates success, but we would argue that any increase is positive. Look deeper, if statistics permit, into your success. Did you reach your target audience? What other groups did you reach? Should you adjust your promotion plan accordingly?

### *Repeat*

Many libraries report a spike in service after a promotional campaign, only to see the increased traffic dwindle. This is common and to be expected. Think about how often over the course of your life you've received promotional letters from any number of publications. We know they are out there, but sometimes we just drift. So, too, do our patrons. So keep reminding them periodically as staff time permits. Enlist new users to talk about your service. Don't be shy – go get 'em!

## Summary

Promoting your IM reference service can be fun! Be creative and enjoy telling folks about the great new service you offer. You can bet that your excitement will be contagious and generate a curious buzz among library patrons! A plan helps execute a successful promotion campaign – one that maximizes resources and reaches target audiences. IM reference is a valuable addition to library services. You know we think so, that's why we wrote this book! So tell everyone about it, and happy IMing!

# References

American Library Association Reference and User Services Association (2004) *Guidelines for Implementing and Maintaining Virtual Reference Services*, MARS Digital Reference Guidelines Ad Hoc Committee; available at: *www.ala.org/ala/rusa/protools/referenceguide/virtrefguidelines.cfm* (accessed: 28 February 2007).

American Library Association Reference and User Services Association (2007) *Measuring and Assessing Reference Services and Resources: A Guide*, RUSA/RSS Evaulation of Reference and User Services Committee; available at: *www.ala.org/ala/rusa/rusaourassoc/rusasections/rss/rsssection/rsscomm/evaluationofref/measrefguide.cfm* (accessed: 12 April 2007).

Bell, J.G. and Levy, A.P. (2004) 'Making the digital connection more personal', in R.D. Lankes, J. Janes, L.C. Smith and C.M. Finneran (eds) *The Virtual Reference Experience: Integrating Theory into Practice*. New York: Neal-Schuman Publishers, pp. 139–61.

Bopp, R.E. (2001) 'The reference interview', in R.E. Bopp and L.C. Smith *Reference and Information Services*. Englewood, CO: Libraries Unlimited.

Boss, R. (undated) 'Virtual reference'; available at: *www.ala.org/ala/pla/plapubs/technotes/virtualreference.cfm* (accessed: 1 May 2007).

Byrnes, J. (2005) 'Nail customer service'; available at: *http://hbswk.hbs.edu/archive/4569.html* (accessed: 29 August 2007).

Casey, M. and Stephens, M. (2007) 'The transparent library: living out loud', *Library Journal*, 132(10): 34.

Coffman, S. (2003) *Going Live: Starting and Running a Virtual Reference Service*. Chicago: American Library Association.

Coffman, S. and Arret, L. (2004a) 'To chat or not to chat – taking another look at virtual reference, part 1', *Searcher*, 12(7); available at: *www.infotoday.com/searcher/jul04/arret_coffman.shtml* (accessed: 3 December 2006).

Coffman, S. and Arret, L. (2004b) 'To chat or not to chat – taking another look at virtual reference, part 2', *Searcher*, 12(8); available at: *www.infotoday.com/searcher/sep04/arret_coffman.shtml* (accessed: 3 December 2006).

Connaway, L.S. and Radford, M.L. (2006) 'The thrill of the chase in cyberspace: a report of focus groups with live chat librarians', *Informed Librarian Online*; available at: *www.informedlibrarian.com/guestForum.cfm?FILE=gf0701.html* (accessed: 1 January 2008).

Crosby, Cathay (2007) Personal e-mail, 23 July.

Fagan, J. (2005) 'Virtual reference software comparative review', *The Charleston Advisor*, 6(4): 16–35.

Fagan, J. and Desai, C. (2002) 'Communication strategies for instant messaging and chat reference services', *The Reference Librarian*, 38(79/80): 121–55.

Ferguson, C.D. and Bunge, C.A. (1997) 'The shape of services to come: values-based reference service for the largely digital library', *College & Research Libraries*, 58(3): 252–65.

Foley, M. (2002) 'Instant messaging reference in an academic library: a case study', *College & Research Libraries*, 63(1): 36–45.

Greer, R. and Grover, R. (1995) 'Libraries as public information utilities: an imperative for survival', unpublished manuscript.

Gross, M., McClure, R. and Lankes, R.D. (2001) 'Assessing quality in digital reference services: overview of key literature on digital reference'; available at: *http://quartz.syr.edu/quality/Reports.htm* (accessed: 2 May 2007).

Janes, J. (2003) *Introduction to Reference Work in the Digital Age*. New York: Neal-Schuman Publishers.

Janes, J. (2004) 'Introduction: the integration of digital reference', in R.D. Lankes, J. Janes, L.C. Smith and C.M. Finneran (eds) *The Virtual Reference Experience: Integrating Theory into Practice*. New York: Neal-Schuman Publishers, pp. 1–7.

Janes, J. and Hill, C. (2002) 'Finger on the pulse: librarians describe evolving reference practice in an increasingly digital world', *Reference & User Services Quarterly*, 42(1): 54–65.

Katz, W.A. (2002) *Introduction to Reference Work: Basic Information Services*, Vol. 1, 8th edn. New York: McGraw-Hill.

Kim, S. and Leem, C. (2005) 'Security of the internet-based instant messenger: risks and safeguards', *Internet Research*, 15(1): 88–98.

Kresh, D. (2002) 'Virtually yours: thoughts on where we have been and where we are going with virtual reference in libraries', *The Reference Librarian*, 38(79/80): 19–34.

Kyrillidou, M. and Young, M. (2006) 'ARL statistics 2004–05: a compilation of statistics from the one hundred and twenty-three members of the Association of Research Libraries'. Washington, DC: Association of Research Libraries.

Lackey, T. (2008) E-mail correspondence with publications and marketing manager, Wyoming State Library, 3 April.

Lipow, A.G. (2002) 'Point-of-need reference service: no longer an afterthought'; available at: *www.ala.org/ala/rusa/protools/futureofref/pointofneed.cfm* (accessed: 28 June 2007).

Lipow, A.G. (2003) *The Virtual Reference Librarian's Handbook*. New York: Neal-Schuman Publishers.

Martin, R.S. (2004) 'Virtual services for real people: building and sustaining a knowledge society', in R.D. Lankes, J. Janes, L.C. Smith and C.M. Finneran (eds) *The Virtual Reference Experience: Integrating Theory into Practice*. New York: Neal-Schuman Publishers, pp. 221–33.

McClure, C., Lankes, R.D., Gross, M. and Choltco-Devlin, B. (2002) 'Statistics, measures and quality standards for assessing digital reference library services: guidelines and procedures'; available at: *http://quartz.syr.edu/quality/Quality.pdf* (accessed: 3 May 2007).

Meola, M. and Stormont, S. (2002) *Starting and Operating Live Virtual Reference Services*. New York: Neal-Schuman Publishers.

Mon, L.M. (2006) 'User perceptions of digital reference services', doctoral dissertation, University of Washington.

Peters, T. and Bell, L. (2006) 'Hello IM, goodbye TTY', *Computers in Libraries*, 26(5): 18–21.

Pew Internet & American Life Project (2008) 'Latest trends – internet adoption'; available at: *http://pewinternet.org/trends/Internet_Adoption_3.18.08[1].pdf* (accessed: 22 February 2008).

Pomerantz, J. (2008) 'Evaluation of online reference services', *Bulletin of the American Society for Information Science and Technology*, 34(2): 15–19.

Radford, M.L. (2003) 'In synch? Evaluating chat reference transcripts', paper presented at Virtual Reference Desk Fifth Annual Digital Reference Conference, San Antonio, Texas, 17–18 November; available at: *http://webjunction.org/do/DisplayContent?id=12666* (accessed: 1 January 2008).

Ronan, J.S. (2003) 'The reference interview online', *Reference & User Services Quarterly*, 43(1): 43–7.

Shiu, E. and Lenhart, A. (2004) 'How Americans use instant messaging'; available at: *www.pewinternet.org/pdfs/PIP_Instantmessage_Report.pdf* (accessed: 22 February 2007).

Shrimplin, A. and Hurst, S. (2007) 'A virtual standoff – using Q methodology to analyze virtual reference', *Evidence Based Library and Information Practice*, 2(4): 4–21.

Steiner, S.K. and Long, C.M. (2007) 'What are we afraid of? A survey of librarian opinions and misconceptions regarding instant messenger', *The Reference Librarian*, 47(1): 31–50.

Straw, J. (2006) 'Using canned messages in virtual reference communication', *Internet Reference Services Quarterly*, 11(1): 39–49.

Strobel, T. (2005) 'If you build it will they come? Marketing strategies to insure success', paper presented at Collaborative Virtual Reference Symposium, 13 July; available at: *www.aclin.org/reference/symposium/2005.html* (accessed: 19 September 2007).

Tucker-Raymond, Caleb (2007) 'Teaching vs giving answers', L-net blog, 18 December; available at: *www.oregonlibraries.net/staff/2007/12/18/teaching_vs_giving_answers* (accessed: 18 December 2007).

Urban Libraries Council (2004) *The Impacts of the Internet on Public Library Use*; available at: *www.urbanlibraries.org/youthsuseoftheinternet.html* (accessed: 22 February 2007).

US Department of Education (1999) *Distance Education at Postsecondary Education Institutions 1997–98*; available at: *http://nces.ed.gov/surveys/peqis/publications/2000013/* (accessed: 2 August 2007).

US Department of Education (2003) *Distance Education at Degree-granting Postsecondary Institutions 2000–01*; available at: *http://nces.ed.gov/surveys/peqis/publications/2003017/* (accessed: 2 August 2007).

Virtual Reference Desk (2003) 'Facets of quality for digital reference services', version 5; available at: *http://data.webjunction.org/wj/documents/11812.pdf* (accessed: 3 September 2007).

# Index

Printed in the United Kingdom by
Lightning Source UK Ltd., Milton Keynes
139879UK00001B/38/P

9 781843 343585